Monday Morning
Soul Missives

An anthology by the
Quiet Rebel Bureau

CONTENTS

Acknowledgments...iii

Introd3uction..1

Grave Dance 5

Light, Camera, Action – Rewrite The Script Of The Film That Is Your Life...........................11

What Will You Choose?..............................18

Your Thinking Is Your Super Power.............26

Begin With Yourself...................................33

Happy Moon Day..39

You Are Limitless 47

Living The Life I Want................................56

Wave the White Flag...................................62

Remember..67

It's Your Choice..73

A Caring Lad Changed My Life 80

Life Is Pretty Good After All 85

What Gives You Joy? 91

My Hidden Children 101

The Space Between Want And Need 109

Happy Monday Namaste 117

From Frustration To Freedom 119

Working For Myself..................................127

Beauty In The Breakdown.........................133

The Disillusioned Lightworker...................138

A Sacred Morning....................................148

Mondays: From Medieval to Magical..........154

You Matter 160

My Love Letter To You 165

An Unexpected Legacy.............................170

About The Authors 181

About The Quiet Rebel Bureau..................201

ACKNOWLEDGMENTS

Thank you to all the authors that made this anthology possible. We couldn't have done it without you.

Monday Morning Soul Missives

INTRODUCTION

Have you ever woken up on a Monday morning and felt the dread of a new week beginning? I know I have. The start of a traditional working week heralds the realisation that there stands 120 hours before you can breathe in the relief of the weekend. That's 7,200 minutes, except for sleep time, that modern-day life expects you to fill. You have work to go to or maybe college courses to take. Families and relationships need to be nurtured and everyday tasks such as shopping must be done. There's travel time, often bumper-to-bumper or sardine-packed on public transport, and occasionally you might be able to fit in a guilt induced trip to the gym. While you participate in the weekly hustle, you're bombarded with information constantly. Turn on your phone and expect to be pinged with social media messages or texts. I bet your email box is full too. Magazines and Instagram shots show perfect bodies with perfect lives, and the subtle message implies that if you don't look picture perfect, you're not trying hard enough. In fact, you're just not enough.

There's no escape; no quietness in our lives. There's no space.

And when Monday morning comes around, the reality of life hits. Where's the joy? Where's the fun and excitement for living? Pressure and stress mounts along with the realisation that time is passing by. Shouldn't there be more to life? Is this it?

All this happens without taking into account your personal difficulties or inner demons that tease or torment you. The way of coping in this world – a world set for the pace of machines, not human beings – is often found in a wine glass, consuming too much or too little food, reaching for a cigarette or switching on the TV to get lost in someone else's drama. How you self-medicate for the pain of modern-day life is self-destructive but for those few moments, it gives the illusion of freedom. You lean on something outside of yourself so you can forget about the pain. The pain is happening on the inside – the pressure of unhappiness and feeling unfulfilled – so reaching for that bottle of whiskey, your drug of choice or your credit card to get those must-have shoes is never going to heal you. It's a temporary numbness and eventually you're going to have to face looking inside for answers.

If you're caught up in dread, dreariness and desperation, you might not believe there's any other answer than to just carry on. Keep breathing, keeping doing what you do and hope nobody can see the emptiness inside. That's not living, it's surviving, and our human potential is far greater than that. But I get how it feels. You feel stuck, you've got responsibilities and you haven't got the confidence to dare to believe that life can change. That YOU can change.

And maybe you listen to the inner, critical voice inside that tells you that you can 't upset the status quo, you can't change. The reasons given by the nagging voice will be varied but based on your fears. It wants to keep you safe and there's perceived safety in staying with the devil you know on grass that's less green than the other side. Who knows that would become of you if you took a step to freeing yourself from pain and unhappiness? Where would *that* crazy adventure lead? Who would you become? Perish the thought that positive change might come out of it. No, better off staying where you are and feeling miserable, while probably hiding it very well.

There comes a time when you can no longer hide it. Cracks appear and stress lines show, maybe you can cover them up with more self-medication but eventually something must give. If you get to this point, that thing that gives is going to be you.

Monday Morning Soul Missives is a collection of letters written to you. They're stories of change and hope. Some letters are deeply personal – from homelessness to childhood incest – bravely shared to show there's light even after facing the darkest of situations. Other letters give you the pep talk you just might need to hear. Perhaps you just need to know that you're not alone and you want proof that other people have jumped off this crazy-speed hamster wheel and found their own bliss in their own way. Life is challenging but it doesn't have to be soul destroying. You don't have to be numb to the world around and inside of you. Read the letters, find your own messages in the book, and be brave enough to believe that there's a beautiful existence waiting for you. Not just on weekends or days off, but even on Mondays too.

Lyn Thurman

Quiet Rebel Bureau

GRAVE DANCE

Jackie Frazier

Dear Reader,

It's Monday morning and you may be thinking, "Blah, my life is dull, boring and uneventful. I keep going around in circles, nothing ever happens, nothing changes." But, it can. A blink of an eye, a decision made on the spur of the moment, even the honk of a horn can change your life from blah to heart fluttering if you grab the moment.

It was a cold, pre-Yule Saturday night in our small, don't blink your eyes or you'll miss it, town. Our town had once been a thriving coal mining town bustling with businesses and people. When the mining fizzled so did our town. Businesses closed and people left. Not much more than a ghost town remained. We didn't even have a McDonalds. The town's only restaurant was a small pizza place owned and operated by an Italian family that had migrated to our community several years prior. They'd stuck it out and remained when other places closed.

A common thing to do on a Saturday night was to drive around and around the town, about a 15-minute circle. Just something that young people did to break the boredom in a town with no entertainment. One Saturday night, my younger sister and I joined the parade. An hour later, nearly dizzy with the constant circling and starting to grow bored, we were ready to call it a night when we spotted a new kid on the block. The 'new kid' was cruising behind the dark tinted windows of a dark metallic green 4x4 truck with desert scenes down each side. Who could it be?

On the third pass, my sister caught me unaware, reached over and honked the horn at the new kid. I couldn't believe she'd done that. We both giggled at her bravery. We circled the town once again. Passing the pizza place, we spied the truck in the parking lot. Lights blinked, code for pull over and let's talk. Should I?

Not to let my sister have all the glory for being brave and daring, I whipped my small truck into the parking lot and pulled up on the driver side of the attention getting green truck. Our windows rolled down simultaneously. Gorgeous deep green eyes met my dark brown ones. I'd been told numerous times that my eyes were dark, mysterious and intriguing. Did he see the mystery and intrigue in them?

He too had someone riding shot gun, his brother. Introductions were made. There was something about those deep green eyes. They were like a tidal wave pulling me down deeper and deeper.

Did my heart flutter?

We ordered a pizza and drinks and got to know each other a little better while sitting on the tailgate of the truck in the moonlight. Norman, the green-eyed truck owner, asked if he and I could meet up after he took his brother home. I agreed.

Finishing off the pizza, we left to take our siblings home. My sister had scored the brother's phone number, so she wasn't too upset that she had to go home. She asked if I thought he'd be there when I got back. There was no doubt in my mind that he'd be there.

An hour later, he helped me into the green truck beside him. No more circling the town for us. With the four-wheel drive engaged, we steadily inched slowly up a mountainside. The road we'd discovered was a one lane, overgrown, dirt road that was nearly invisible in the darkness.

Barely able to see where we were going, I wouldn't have been surprised to have looked out to find us driving through the air of the dark night sky. After what seemed forever, the road came to an end at the edge of what appeared to be a forgotten graveyard. Leaving the headlights burning, we stepped down from the truck into what felt like another dimension, another world, another time. Had the overgrown dirt road been a portal?

Norman came around the truck and took my hand. A tingle travelled through my fingertips straight to my heart, electrifying. I looked into his eyes. I felt like I was drowning in the dark green depth of those eyes each time I dared to glance deeply into them. In quiet awe, we walked among the headstones which were large standing rocks with hand chiselled, weather worn names and dates that were barely readable. The stones reminded me of Stonehenge. Maybe we'd travelled into another time and place.

The air seemed to stir softly. I watched as Norman gently caressed several of the headstones. I sensed a spiritual connection between him and the souls that lay beneath them. The connection travelled through the stones, his hands and into me. After visiting each grave, we made our way to the outer edge of the graveyard.

He asked me to wait while he returned to the truck were, he pulled out a basket and shut off the headlights. The glow of the full moon filtered through the trees, guiding him back to me. Like a magician, he pulled a blanket, a radio, candles and a bottle of wine from the basket.

Did my heart flutter?

A click had country love songs filling the dark quietness. Had I heard a sigh other than my own? Candles filled the air with their perfumed scent while adding flickering light to that of the moon. Sitting on the warm, soft blanket, we talked softly and wondered curiously about those we shared the night with as we passed the bottle of wine between us. Was there a reason for us, two people who had just met, to be there on this night?

Removing my shoes, I stood and reached for his hand. "Will you dance with me?" I asked. He too removed his shoes. His warm calloused hands closed around mine.

Did my heart flutter?

Just as our barefoot dance began, large diamond crusted snowflakes began to fall from the night sky joining our dance. Weaving amongst the headstones, we stopped at each with an invitation to dance. Soon wispy, grey shapes swirled with the falling snow joining our magical dance on this once forgotten snow covered mountaintop.

Did my heart flutter?

Three decades ago, I was going around and around in circles on a dull, boring night when a honk of a horn and a spur of the moment decision changed my life forever. I chose to break the circle and grab the moment. The decision led to a barefoot dance on a snow-covered mountain top with a green-eyed stranger.

Today, Norman and I still share a bottle of wine, memories of that most magical night and a pre-Yule dance on a forgotten graveyard that we inherited when we purchased our property. If we're lucky, we dance barefoot in the snow.

Does my heart flutter? Yes.

An unknown author wrote, "Don't be afraid to the take the unfamiliar path. Sometimes they're the ones that take your heart places." Life was never meant to blah.

LIGHT, CAMERA, ACTION – REWRITE THE SCRIPT OF THE FILM THAT IS YOUR LIFE

Sandra ten Hoope

Dear Reader,

It's Monday morning and you've hit that snooze button over and over and over and over. Five minutes more. Just five minutes more. Monday songs razing through your muddled mind. None promise a positive outcome. You're dreading the day ahead. A new day of going through the motions, bypassing your emotions.

If only you could stay in bed, go back to sleep. Embrace that wonderful parallel-self that you encounter occasionally in your dreams. The one that HAS a life ... if only it were Sunday again. Snooze alarm, snooze alarm ... not ready to leave the twilight zone and step into the B-movie that your life has become.

Mundane Monday

Why do Mondays get such a bad rap in songs? Could it be that Monday has become a synonym for ´reality´? A reality where there is little or no room for our dreams.

Dreams that we once, when we were little, had in abundance. What will I become? Where will I live? With whom? Will I have children? We would fantasise for hours and hours in a world that presented itself to us as an oyster. With ourselves as the hidden shiny gem.

Most of our dreams however never materialised. As we grew older, we were pushed into being `realistic`. Forced to be sensible, to choose the safe road. Our pearl slowly lost its shine.

We forgot about being an astronaut or a ballerina. Playtime soon was over, it was time to face the real world. A world in which ultimately everything seemed real. But you! The real you got swamped by convention. Found herself lost in unwritten, restricting rules.

So, you settled. For less. For something else than you envisaged. Your passions subsided. Your drive shrunk. Your dreams vanished, lost their shine, got parked in the shades. Lacking light. Lacking a zest for life. Making you feel like everybody else. Mundane middle of the road. Or even worse, like a nobody.

That's what reality did to you. Made you drive on the middle of the road. In the words of Will Smith: `Being realistic is the most common path to mediocrity`. But you did not land on this planet to lead a mediocre life. You're here to shine.

Dare it Up

What if you would turn the camera on you? Dared to believe again? Believe that there is life beyond this mediocre state of survival? Believe that you can break free from the boing chains of the 9 to 5, which only provides a false sense of security? For the real security lies within you. In your passion. In your skills. Believe that Mondays can be fun days?

If only you would dare. Dare to displease. For stepping out into your light may well cause others to be displeased, which scares us. From an early age on, women are wired to please others. Parents, siblings, teachers, friends, anybody really. All we wished for was to be seen as ´good´ girls. Good was the norm. A norm we overstepped whenever we wanted to be anything other than just pretty or nice. Whenever we allowed our dreams to surface, our surroundings made us push these back. Keeping us small.

But here you are now. Displeasing yourself.

Every single day. By not doing a job you truly love. Or by not being with a person that loves you for who you really are. The parallel-you that you meet in your dreams, that keeps you from waking up in the morning, she is knocking on your soul. Harder and harder. Screaming at you: BELIEVE. Look at yourself. Take that selfie of your soul. Turn that camera on the one person who deserves your attention more than anybody in this world: you! Allow yourself to believe that you're worthy of anything you once dreamed of. She knows: no woman should ever live a should-driven life! Ready? Take a deep breath and then ...

Light, Camera, Action

Take 1 – Driver's or rather, director's seat

Smell the coffee (regular, soy or bulletproof) and make an inventory of anything and anybody that's keeping you from living a life that pleases you. Your mum, your manager, your partner, your finances, your limited beliefs. All the things that went wrong. That you did wrong (or so you think). This isn't an overview to showcase on social media. It's for you and for you alone. For only if you acknowledge where you are right now can you plan ahead.

Once the overview is ready, allow yourself some quiet time. Look at every person, every situation, every action, every reaction – look at all this with compassion and curiosity. Life is like a film – a collection of scenes. In a film, the director dictates the setting. He controls

14

the lens. If he were to take a different viewpoint, shed a different light, add different music, the scene would be completely different. Now see if you can look back at past scenes and change the perspective. Change the lines. Change the light. Change the actors. Change your part in it all. Is it as set in stone as you thought? Or, is there room for another perspective? And if so, room for (self)forgiveness?

We can't stop life from happening. A director will do as many takes as he deems necessary. We lack that luxury, but we can go back and rewrite the script, reset our memory. Change the outcome – not of the situation, but of how you perceive it. Do add notes to self on how to handle future scenes more in alignment with your soul. For you're the director of your life.

Take 2 – AcoPLAYlipse now

So, now we've experienced playing with memories. Let´s play some more.

Dig deep into your past: what kind of activity sparked you up when you were a child? Sports, dancing, being with your friends, arts and crafts? For in those memories, in those forgotten dreams and desires you will find the answer. You will find the key to set free your inner child, who is still there. Hidden but for sure not gone. Ready to run outside and play as soon as you open the door.

Now take one of these activities and allow yourself five minutes a day to enjoy it. Five minutes is all it takes. Trust me, it will reset your system. Let the joy of doing what you love, surprise and awaken you. Those five minutes may grow into more minutes. You may also add other five-minute activities – it's your day, your film, you direct its course. Tracking your accomplishments will keep you motivated, and it serves as part of a gratitude journal, which has been proven to increase happiness.

Take 3 – Onwards to the Oscars

Armed with tools to rewrite memories and re-find joy, let´s set you up for the next step. Allowing for plot-twists (you know budget reductions, roadworks, accidents, going down with a cold, co-actors throwing tantrums), write the perfect script. The choice is yours – will the film span a year, two years? Do you have a sequel or trilogy in mind? Some love short-term planning and others go for the long-game. What has worked for many: dream big, act small. By means of a vision board, set the mood for long term goals in the areas of business, family, housing and travelling. Break all goals down into small, actionable steps. Tick these off as you go along. Do not overcommit yourself: films take years to make – planning, financing, the actual shooting, post-production. Allow yourself space and do tap into your feelings regularly. Do the goals still make your soul sing? Remember, it's YOUR film. Your life. You may change your mind. Take out your calendar and mark each first Monday of the month as Made it Work Monday. On which, you celebrate all the ticked boxes and rewrite goals to YOUR pleasing – which will in time lead to the One Big Box Office Success: the new, snooze-free YOU. Do send me an invite to the Gala Premiere!

WHAT WILL YOU CHOOSE?

Wendy Radford

Dear Reader,

Well hello to you.... it's Monday morning and I must own up to the fact that I'm feeling very excited. I have some news for you that I think you'll find uplifting. I know...some of you just want to crawl back into bed and pull the covers over your head, already longing for the weekend. The rest of you may be waking up full of excitement and anticipation of an exciting new day. However, either way, don't go back to bed. Stay with me for a moment and let's have a chat.

Life can be wonderful every day and I'm going to share with you what I discovered over the weekend. I think it just might change your way of viewing the start of your weeks forever.

How cool would that be? Starting each day with renewed vim, vigour and awe?

It starts with a firm decision to step out of the traditional Monday morning box and decide to take a fresh approach. It's choosing to see every day as a chance to create/see something wonderful and magical. It doesn't matter how large or small. It can be just one bodacious, magical experience or thought each day.

Draw on your faith, your intuition and knowledge of life to do this. Set the intention that your day will be joyful no matter what's going on around you. Plant the seed that you'll be enchanted by something by the end of the day. In releasing your negative judgments, you can expand your vision of life. This is experimental.... using different ways to try things.

Know that you can't fail, for every day in every way you are growing spiritually, whether you're aware of it or not. Trust yourself and listen to the positive music and melody of your life. There is no such thing as a mistake, just a bringing of lessons and opportunities to move forward. What you learn each day is immeasurable when you're looking for the fantastical.

Your first wonderful creation? Understand, Dear Reader, that it's how you choose to see/view things that is the critical point. There are 360 degrees of feelings and emotions you can choose to experience...180 fabulous...Yippy!...180 rubbish.... Bother. Or words to that effect.

It's always your choice which way you choose to go. It's about focus. Focus requires you to be fully engaged in the present moment. Claim your wisdom... decide to thrive not just survive. Take that leap of faith and get out of bed with joy in your heart and make time to stay with me just a little time longer.

Let's discuss the word joy before we get to much further on with our Monday morning. There are two forms of joy. There's the ego-based joy that comes and goes and is dependent on external conditions and situations. Then there's soul joy, which is a totally different experience. Soul joy offers a sense of peace no matter what. It's lasting, as it doesn't rely on anything external. It comes from within you. It's freedom to let go of fear and doubt with nothing to prove and being your true self in honesty and truth.

With this knowledge and a little practise, you can learn the difference between true lasting joy and soul nourishment compared with ego-based joy, which is always short lived and seeks outside confirmation.

Seek no explanation or permission from others to be in joy. Sometimes people will tell you to go with your gut reaction. However, the gut reactions come from a place of fear. While you're focusing and dependent on the outside world to feel joyful, you're giving away your personal power. You're strongly in the ego story of victimhood. So, Dear Reader, which joy are you going to choose to bring forward as you get out of bed this morning? Dial up the trust in yourself to high, stretch your boundaries. Remember, it's your choice which way you see your day. Your soul response always comes from love.

Now that you're out of bed Dear Reader, with joy in your own heart, let's look at the things that might come up to bite you and knock you off your joy filled pillar. It can be anything: a lost slipper, alarm didn't go off, no hot water, run out of coffee, can't find the jumper you want...must finish this article, etc. All very little things in the grand scheme of things, however, this can be enough to trigger your ego. The voice in your head that says can't, won't, must, need, ought, should, could, would...sound familiar?

However, if you choose, you can see this as a sign from the universe asking you to take that leap of faith and to look at things differently. To see each of these things as a learning curve, an opportunity to release your reaction to these tiny blips and to avoid being provoked in your day. To choose to... instead of playing the usual triangle of victim, rescuer and perpetrator, calling forward a new way of responding.

This triangle I've just mentioned happens inside our heads nearly every minute of every day. Sometimes it happens so quickly, we don't even know we're still playing the game. Equally, we also invite other people to join us in the game, to be our partners in pain, thereby reinforcing our victim belief. When we interfere with the path of another or allow another to interfere with us without being asked, we're playing the dance of the triangle.

So, what can you do? You can choose a new response, take that leap of faith and encourage the ego victim to transform into your inner teacher, the abuser corner to become the mentor and the rescuer to transcend into a healer. So, we can now see how every moment of every day is a new and exciting chance to choose how we wish to see our lives. Do we wish to just survive, or do we want to thrive? Trust that you're good enough and that you deserve to be happy and express your truth. Learn to expand not contract. You don't have to change anything in your life, except your view of it.

The art of watching our thoughts, Dear Reader, is the very first step to finding internal joy. So, let's consider a benevolent thought. It's a way of finding beauty in our lives. A benevolent thought doesn't question itself, nor would it ever leave you or anyone else feeling less than, nor would it judge, nor would it share anything that would not leave another feeling uplifted. This, Dear Reader, is how to start your Monday morning, making sure that your thoughts are benevolent thoughts.

Benevolence is a form of love. With love comes freedom. An equation can look like this

Love+Trust =Joy =Freedom

Love is a huge umbrella word Dear Reader and we brandish it around willy-nilly...I love my car...I love roses...I love chocolate...I love dancing oh, and by the way, I love you. Where about in that line up do I come in? Above chocolate yet below your car? See what I mean? It's a very large word that gets over used these days. True love will only exist when there is trust. If you remove trust, there can only be love left and that's heavy and will feel out of balance. In this energy, a person can be left feeling less than, put upon, used, tired etc I'm sure you get the drift of this. If you take away love and there is only trust, this would be equally out of sync. When you can relax and remember that trust and love are both needed to be present simultaneously, your heart will begin to open to your true benevolence and life will be seen through a different magical lens.

For those who say they've lived in trust and love and have got badly burned, I challenge them to look deep and ask, "Was love and trust truly present and being expressed?" So, if we look at the equation again, can you see Dear Reader that if you're coming from the benevolent form of love and trust, you'll find your internal joy that brings a true feeling of freedom to enjoy life?

In my travels, I recently came across this little poem that I'd love to share with you. I think it really can sum up each of us on some morning or other, not just Monday mornings.

A poem from ANON

Dear God,
So far today I've done all right.
I haven't gossiped. I haven't lost my temper.
I haven't been greedy, moody, nasty, selfish or
narcissistic.
And I'm glad about that.
But in a few minutes, god, I'm going to get out
of bed,
And from then on, I'm going to need a bit more
help.
Thank you.
Amen

Tomorrow morning as you open your eyes, put you hand on your heart, start a new leaf in the book of your life, start a new chapter and choose to find benevolent thoughts where ever you are. Recognise life as a series of magical opportunities to come from love and bring forward your internal teacher. Recognise your own inner mentor and receive your own healing energy, which is deep inside you. Find your own unique and very bountiful joy. Look for the beauty in others, look beyond their ego and find their soul. Do this without seeking the need to be 'special', and you will gain your own individual joy filled Monday mornings. To be fair, from now on, you can make every morning of the week just as uplifting, exciting and magical as this Monday morning is now going to be. So, be enchanted, trust in the good of all. It really is a lovely time to be alive and on this beautiful planet.

Go forth Dear Reader and spread your love, light and wisdom through benevolent thoughts all day. Thank you and bless you for spending this time with me. I love, honour and respect you always. Please, remember that all is truly well and smile.

S = signal
M = my
I = intention
L = to love
E = everyone

SMILE Dear Reader and love and light will radiate from you all day. Rejoice you are alive. Yippy! Happy Monday!

YOUR THINKING IS YOUR SUPER POWER

Martine Bolton

Dear Reader,

It's Monday morning and today I'd like to remind you that your thinking is your superpower!

Our thoughts are so foundational to our happiness and success in life, yet relatively few of us are good, positive, free thinkers.

Conversely, many of us are good over-thinkers, worriers and self-doubters that hold on to fears, faulty beliefs and 'knowledge' that really don't help us. Yet, the quality of our thinking is foundational to the quality of our lives and the results that we create.

The most fundamental difference between

the person sleeping homeless on the street and the likes of Richard Branson or Oprah Winfrey is in the quality and constructiveness of their thinking. So, it's not JUST thinking that differentiates the successful from the unsuccessful - our health, habits, actions and decisions also play a big part - but it's our thinking that drives our emotions, which impact our health, which affects our drive and energy, which influences our actions, which impact our relationships and behavioural choices, which determine the results that we get! So, it all starts with a thought. Good, clear, constructive thinking leads to excellent results. When we think well, we do well.

So many of us pick up negative and limiting beliefs about ourselves, other people, life, the universe and everything, and these beliefs can be disruptive and disabling. We pick these ideas up from faulty information that we're given, lies that we're told and faulty assumptions that we make based on our experiences and how we're treated.

According to a study by *Psychology Today*, 60 – 70 per cent of the average person's thinking is negative. Interestingly, most of us believe that our thinking is 60 -70 per cent positive, which would imply that much of the time we're probably not even aware of what or how we're thinking.

Whatever the percentages, it's probably reasonable to suggest that most of us have a fair bit of unhelpful or faulty thinking and 'programming' that, if we're not careful, can stop us from being as happy, healthy, successful and prosperous as we might otherwise be. This is because thoughts are highly creative in their nature, and what we think about, we tend to bring about.

Thinking is the CAUSE...

Outcomes are the EFFECT

With our thinking, we can either find ourselves living the life of our dreams, or that of our worst nightmares. But herein lies freedom. By becoming more conscious moment to moment of what's going on in our minds, we can learn to take control and direct our thinking to stay focused on what we want. This helps us to bring about more of the positive outcomes that we want and less of the negative outcomes that we don't want.

We live in an almost constant stream of thought, and these thoughts aren't always calm, clear, logical and rational. We confuse beliefs with facts. Our beliefs are self-fulfilling (even if untrue). We are largely fear-based (it's a survival instinct), meaning that many of our thoughts are negative. Much of what we think we 'know' is faulty or limited in its truth. We delete / distort / generalise and make other thinking errors. We're biased. We create problems for ourselves that aren't there. We project faulty 'learning' from the past onto the present, creating repetitive scenarios. We believe our thinking, and whatever our beliefs, we usually think they're right.

Because we're not always aware of our thinking in the moment, it can be helpful to monitor our feelings, as these alert us to what we're thinking.

So today, if you catch yourself feeling any emotion that doesn't feel good, I would like to invite you to try some or all the following:

- Recognise that worry, fear, doubt and all other forms of negative and unhelpful thinking act like kryptonite to our systems – weakening us, draining our energy and rendering us unresourceful.

- Take conscious control of your breathing.

- Slow down (even thinking the words "Slow down..." helps to put you in a calmer, more resourceful thinking state).

- If the bad feeling is one of stress due to demands, ask yourself: "What two or three things must I absolutely get done today?" followed by, "What's the thing that I should start right now?" Then, do one thing at a time (FOCUS - Follow One Course Until Successful). Tell yourself "I always have more than enough time to do what's most important". This is an excellent belief to hold in life and it will help you to feel calmer and more in control. For most of us, the work is never done, so don't pressurise yourself to clear your in-box every day. Your priority should always be your wellbeing (followed by the wellbeing of your loved ones, and then your work – in that order). You can't pour from an empty vessel.

- If the bad feeling is in response to something that's happened, ask yourself: "What thought am I thinking that's creating this feeling? What judgements, assumptions and conclusions have I made? Might I be distorting, deleting, or making generalisations here? Is there another way of looking at this? What's a better, more constructive thought to hold?"

- It's important to consider what you want (in terms of the best outcome possible), and what you will need to do or say next, to make that happen. This helps you to stay focused on the bigger picture and what's important in the longer term.

- Mantras or affirmations are really soothing in difficult situations and can help to see you through all kinds of adversity. Here are just a few of my favourites...

    - I've got this
    - Whatever happens, I'll handle it
    - This situation is quickly and easily resolved for the highest good of all concerned
    - I could see peace instead of this
    - I am safe, I am loved, and all is well

- Things are always working out for me
- I am whole; perfect; strong; powerful; loving; harmonious; and happy.

- Meditation is a wonderful activity for the mind, which also has many benefits for the body. It enables us to see our thoughts from a detached perspective, and to become less reactive and more considered in our responses. Even 10-15 minutes in the mornings before we do anything else can make a big difference.

- Visualisation is a powerful technique that can help us achieve the results we desire. Think of this as movies that you play over in your mind. Building up a clear mental image of what you want, and then holding that image in your mind regularly and for as long as you can, helps to impress an image on the subconscious part of your mind, which then goes into action to help you turn your visualisations into reality in the material world. Visualisation becomes even more powerful when you add good feelings into the mix, re-creating the good, positive feelings you'll experience once you've achieved your goal(s). Many of the most successful people in the world attribute their success – at least in part - to the power of positive thinking, and specifically to the use of visualisation.

In summary, please remember today that your thinking is your superpower. Learn to direct it more consciously and effectively, avoid the kryptonite of worry, fear and doubt, and you'll have all the tools you need to create a happy, healthy, successful and prosperous life.

All power to you.

BEGIN WITH YOURSELF

Kate May

Dear Reader,

Its Monday morning and the weekend's over, but this doesn't mean you've got to have the usual Monday morning blues. You're alive. You have breath in your body and love in your soul. Whilst it's down to you to motivate yourself, I'd love to inspire you.

How do you rate your life? Ten out 10? Eight out of 10? Even less? I score a 10 out of 10 on the happiness chart. I'm completely happy in my personal life, my family life, my working life, my home and with my financial income. I'm very fortunate in many ways. Whilst I do appreciate this is easy for me now and harder for others, I've created the life I want.

I used to be at a five out of five. I went to work and was a real jobsworth, making other people's lives a misery. I'm sure life wasn't completely crap, I had a five after all. The evenings and most of my twenties were a blur as I rocked the 90s. I had a good job and good friends. I made loads of amazing memories, but I was always searching for something else. I wasn't fulfilled.

My spiritual journey was on and off for many years, mainly due to my awakening or more to the point, the fact that it wasn't quite awakened. There were hints it would be, but then a night out on the town (I did say it was the 1990s) always seemed to use up my cash, leaving little left for the mindfulness courses my soul ached for. Eventually, I had the awakening: what if I were nicer to people? What if, instead of being a jobsworth, I helped people? This took a little effort before it became second nature. I found that instead of getting annoyed when I was in another queue for stamps, I'd look at the scenery or I'd text a friend. I would make the best out of each situation.

It wasn't long before people helped me back. I no longer had to face bitchy shop assistants. I faced kind ones instead and that helped me. I joined a spiritual group and met new friends, and very slowly I changed. What I realised was that my actions had cause and effect, karma. My energy attracted the energy that came back to me. Do you know how powerful that is? That makes us magical.

Fast forward several years and several

homes later, including living la vida loca in Spain. I'm still a five out of 10. Not good enough. My spiritual awakening was really starting to happen, and I could feel that I needed to change more. My inner peace was calling, and I was well on my way to answering. I left an unfulfilling but well-paid job to have my family. This was a turning point in my life, as I felt much happier inside and out. But this only made me a six out of 10. My finances suffered but I was happier. I chose to do jobs I enjoyed in order to bring in a few extra pennies for what I needed, and I changed my lifestyle of regular shopping trips for simpler things. I joined a mother and baby group, and I was asked if I would like to do treatments on the mums (I'd trained as a beauty therapist many moons before). This hobby turned into weekly work for me, which allowed me to pay for the extra kids clubs the mums all went to. There's a bigger story here, but in a nut shell, it's how I ended up being a tarot reader.

Working with Spirit, I learnt to find that inner peace even more. Everything started to fall into place, and it wasn't long before I was running my own business. I had regular clients, I set up mind-body-spirit fayres and I wrote for different spiritual magazines. Work wise, I was very happy. My personal life, however, was a different matter. After 15 years of marriage, I left my husband. After years of being in a marriage that wasn't working – the arguments, the pain we caused each other, the dread of going home for both of us, the lies, and the deceit – I couldn't go on anymore. He was never going to change, so I did. I chose to be a single mum of two children, and this made me a nine out of 10. How quick was that? I re-built my life and took my career even further. I met a wonderful man and fell deeply in love with everything. Life was good but was about to change yet again.

More recently, I was pushed out of an environment in which I had built many friendships and part of my career around. This dropped me to an eight out of 10. This sudden change meant I had to trust Spirit and what plans were meant to be. This was one of the best things that could have happened to me. I created a new place, new friendships and realised that the previous environment was stifling me in more ways than I'd known. I was now in a ten out of 10 place.

I have purposely not included my wonderful current relationship because I don't believe I need to be in this to be ten out of 10. However, just for the record, that's also a perfect 10. We respect each other, and we have very similar beliefs. I fancy the pants off him. If I could write a top ten list of men, he would be on the top of it.

Where am I now? I own my own spiritual coffee shop and psychic development centre, Mystic River Lounge, in Cosham, Portsmouth with my best friend, Paula. I travel twice a year to California with my partner Colin, doing readings and workshops. I teach the tarot at the centre and run a weekly psychic development class. The coffee shop is booming, and we have the most wonderful customers. I'm making lots of new friends and I'm strengthening bonds with old ones. I help run more than five large mind-body-spirit fayres and have a regular flow of clients each week. I work in London at Selfridges with the Psychic Sisters doing readings. I blog, I vlog, and I write monthly tarot/psychic scopes. My children have adapted perfectly with the changes and enjoy time with me and with their dad on weekends. They love coming to the shop after school with their friends for milkshakes and doughnuts.

I've achieved all this by making changes in just the last three years. I'm happy and have inner peace. Every day fills me with excitement, and I laugh lots. I can see the positive in most things and enjoy the simple things like a lazy Sunday watching Netflix in PJs on the sofa with my family.

If I can do this so can you – why not? What's stopping you? You are. The two or more numbers that stop you getting to that 10 are your blocks. Energy works by gravitation, and what you allow yourself to focus on will increase that energy. If you allow those missing numbers into your life, they'll hold energy – the wrong energy, the missing fulfilment energy. If you're accepting eight out of 10, focus is on that missing two.

Appreciate the little things. Look at the cup half full, not half empty. What can you do to move this to 10 out of 10? Make the changes today – see yourself in two years, five years, or 10 years – where do you want to be? What do you want to be? Who do you want to be?

For me, turning 40 was a huge milestone. I couldn't be in a loveless marriage for another 10 years. One day, I pulled a tarot card at work: it was the hermit, so I went home and ended the marriage there and then. It may sound crazy but sometimes you must do crazy things to be happy.

On this wonderful day that you've woken up alive, you can change your life and no longer have those Monday blues. Be excited for each day. Notice the wind, sun, stars, leaves, insects and birds. Be happy with yourself, kind to others, give love where you can, but first begin with yourself.

HAPPY MOON DAY

Sarah Robinson

Dear Reader,

It's Monday morning and the day of the moon.

My suggestion to make your Monday luminous is to treat it as was done in ancient times. A moon day devoted to connecting to the goddess and energy of the moon. Drawing on moon energy can help illuminate a path of comfort and joy to help you find your way on the darkest of mornings. The moon is a calming constant that we can all call upon, like the earth and the sky.

The name Monday comes from Old English meaning day of the moon. Monday is also moon day in other languages including Spanish, German, Norwegian, French,

Japanese and Thai. The moon may well be our oldest method of telling time, with its waxing and waning rhythms outlining lunar months. It has also long been connected with the divine feminine and feminine cycles (isn't it interesting that the cooler, changeable faces of the moon are easier to use to identify the monthly cycles than the bright light of the sun? Sometimes the gentler approach works best!).

The rhythms of the earth and the universe are ever moving; years, seasons, weeks, days. These many spirals have a magic all their own and one you can connect to should you choose. Finding the gifts in each moment, you can treat Monday as a moon day in many beautiful ways: You can honour the goddesses of the moon. You can treat Monday as a full-moon day, set intentions and connect to the ancient meanings of the moon.

Monday as full moon day

Each Monday, we're gifted a beautiful new day. Pristine, constant, like pearls strung upon a necklace. Thread by goddesses, a string of beautiful moon beads. These Monday pearls might look a lot like little round full moons. And it's very possible that Mondays can feel like a full moon day to you; a time when many people feel heightened emotions. You may feel a little extra sensitive. So, what if you treated every Monday like a full moon day, a perfect time to release the old and move forward into new light?

This can be a time to let go of fear and anxiety, to forgive and start afresh. and to carry what you are grateful for forward with you into your next steps (Once or twice a year the full moon does fall on Monday. Treat these days and yourself with extra reverence and care).

Name your moon: intentions

Each lunar month's moon has its own beautiful name inspired by the month such as snow moon, harvest moon and flower moon. You can draw on this idea and name your moon-day Monday with an intention to inspire your day. At the beginning of yoga classes, and often for new moons, we set an intention for the times ahead to inspire, connect and guide our thoughts.

So, each Monday, think of a word, phrase or emotion that you'd like to channel for the week. Feel free to say it aloud, write it down and pin it to a mirror, meditate, or light a candle for it. Perhaps a *Calm Monday,* a *Friendship Monday*, a *Joyful Monday*, or *Self-Care Monday*, or indeed any word or phrase that resonates with you (I'm all for *Jazzy New Shoes Monday* or *I'm Eating Two Croissants For Breakfast Monday*).

Why connect to the moon and her goddess archetypes?

If you work towards discovering your unique

connection to the moon, you can connect to healing and empowerment as well as find harmony within your own nature. Taking time to acknowledge or reflect on the moon is an acknowledgement of the cycles we embody and live within. Connecting to the moon can help you to acknowledge and recognise your own cycles and changing needs, a lunar reminder to listen to your intuition. Honour your sensitivity rather than seeing it as a weakness, this is how you can find balance and harmony.

Which goddesses do you connect with and why? Do you feel inspired to channel certain goddesses to help bring you strength or inspiration? Are they acting as way markers for an area you feel you need to grow in such as self-love or compassion? There are no rules for connecting to the goddesses. Doing it in your own way will help you find greater peace, strength and self-love. Blessed be.

Ideas from eight sacred moon goddesses.

Here are some simple ideas to bring joy to your Monday as inspired by the qualities of eight awesome moon goddesses. With their lanterns filled with soft moonlight, the Goddesses can guide us though dark days. They can help us find joy, inspiration, direction and comfort in the ever-spinning wheel of the year.

- Arianrhod (Celtic) is goddess of the moon and stars. Her name means silver- wheel and the spinning wheel weaving the tapestry of our lives. What small threads can you weave to create a beautiful tapestry for your day, week or year? Take time to journal about your goals and dreams or create a vision board.

- Kerridwen (Celtic) and her cauldron symbolise the transformative power of magic, wisdom and rebirth.
  You can use Kerridwen's cauldron to let go of what may be holding you back. Write down fears, anxieties, jealousies, grudges or anything you wish to let go of on a piece of paper. Scrunch it up and throw it into a pot or cauldron and burn it (you can do this in real life or in a meditation).

- Chandi (Hindu) is the female counterpart to Chandra, lord of the Moon. Chandi is fierce, powerful, and known by many names such as Great Magic and She Who Is Without Fear. There are many stories about this goddess. My favourite is the one about Chandi and Chandra taking it in turns to be the moon. One month, Chandi becomes the moon and the next, Chandra fulfils the role. So even this fearsome and powerful goddess sees the value in taking time to rest and share roles. To ask for help isn't weakness but strength. It takes strength to

43

release ownership and take time for yourself. What tasks can you let go of? What tasks can you delegate to others? What activities are no longer serving you?

- Kuan Yin (Chinese) is a Buddhist goddess and protectress, goddess of the moon, compassion, and healing. She's the embodiment of love and kindness. It's said she hears the cries of all the beings of earth.
Can you listen to what you need today? A nourishing meal? A walk in nature or a good chat with a friend? Think about how you can treat yourself with compassion today. Kuan Yin suggests that the way to release suffering is through compassion for self and others, so try to release judgement or criticism of how the day went and send love to yourself for making it through the day!

- Rhiannon (Celtic) is the goddess of fertility and the moon. Her name means divine queen and her affinity for horses represents her love of freedom and authenticity.
Celebrate the night and channel your inner queen with a warm bath, candles and scented oils. You've made it through the day. Enjoy a few sweet luxuries to unwind and settle into a restful evening. It's time to be free, time to let go of the burdens you've carried and roles you've played during the day and just enjoy being you.

- Hina (Hawaiian). Hina started life as a mortal woman but grew weary of the noises and stresses of the earth. She retreated to the moon to find peace and calm (I think we can all relate to that) and from her moon perch she helps guide sailors across the ocean.
You may not be able to retreat to the moon, but you can find a retreat space today, even if it's just for 10 minutes. A yoga class, a meditation in a quiet room, a cup of tea in a cosy chair. Channel Hina as you take time for yourself so that you can help others when they need you.

- Xochhiquetzal (Aztec). This powerful goddess is connected with the concepts of beauty, fertility, crafts, dance, music and magic. She's a protector of women and a dual goddess of sun and moon. Channel Xochhiquetzal and take joy in creating your own little magic with love today. Dance or chant to your own rhythm or create a story, song or poem to tell your loved ones before bed.

- Diana (Roman) carries a silver bow for hunting under the moonlight. She is the goddess of the hunt, powerful and focused.
Every day take an action towards your goals, no matter how small. Never lose sight of what is important to you. Mondays can involve moving to other people's timetables and schedules. However, remember that you're in

charge of your path. Don't let go of your dreams, dearest warrior goddess.

In addition to these lovely goddesses, there is a notable god I'd like to mention;

Norse moon god Mani. His story is that each night he pulls the moon across the sky, trying to escape and save it from a mythological wolf. Should this wolf ever catch them, it would tear the moon to pieces and the world would end.

Know that whatever happens on this Monday, even if you feel tired or falter, it's not the end of days. The earth will continue to turn, and you'll have a chance to start afresh, forgive, and try again.

In finding a connection, whether that be with the moon, myth, nature, magic or other, we can find hand holds to grasp onto for support on challenging days. Without connection, we can feel lost, untethered and insecure. So, go forth and explore. Strengthen the bonds with that which brings you joy and set loose that which drags you down. It's a journey, not of rules but of heart and soul, moon and magic. A never-ending voyage. Take your time and find your way through the cycles in your own beautiful, unique way. Your Monday is a chance to set how you'd like your week to go. Claim your moon day and the week will be a beautiful one.

You are always blessed with moonbeams, even when you cannot see them.

Merry moon day x

YOU ARE LIMITLESS

Charlotte Chase

Dear Reader,

Here's the truth. You're enough, you're worthy and if you choose, you're limitless. I know what you're thinking, "That's easy for you to say."

Not so long ago, just a few years ago in fact, my life was a mess. I'd gone from job to job, always thinking maybe the next one will be 'the one'. I was in destructive relationships. After each disappointment I'd find, yet again, I was feeling the same emptiness. I always stayed in each job and relationship for a year or so, because the guilt took over, the fear of what to do next. Could I leave? Was I letting people down?

Now I see that you're never stuck, really.

47

Honestly, feeling stuck is just a by-product of the choices you make. You see, we only ever really have two choices in life. Stay where we are and accept it or change it. It's just all the 'stuff' we add on top that gets in our way. The what ifs, what will people think, what if I fail, what if I succeed, what if the grass isn't greener? Is any of this sounding familiar?

I'll take you back to my teens because I feel these years have a huge impact on our lives and what direction and path we choose later in life. Of course, we all have the power to change our circumstances and use any difficult experiences for growth. My depression started young, I can't quite pinpoint where to be honest. I was always anxious and painfully shy. I didn't make friends easily and I was so desperate to be accepted. If I did make friends, I became a massive people-pleaser and tried to be what I thought people wanted me to be. I couldn't deal with any form of conflict. As you can imagine, this made me a great target growing up, so conflict was exactly what I experienced. I can't really say that I ever felt like I found my place growing up. I felt lost and confused and like I didn't quite fit in with any social group. I ended up in the rebel crowd when I was 12 and in trouble a lot at school, half of the time for things I didn't do. So, I accepted the role I was labelled with at school and went with it. My heart knew better, so I ended up as the quiet one of the rebels. I was scared, a complete pushover and felt like the outcast even in my friendship circle.

The first day of college, I decided 'this is it'.

This is my chance to reinvent myself. I was so excited at the prospect that I didn't have to be me. I could be anyone I wanted to be. Even though I came over full of confidence and extremely self-assured, it was a complete lie. In fact, my anxiety and depression were already spiralling out of control. With the added stress of problems at home, which I pretended were not even happening, I started not to cope. I began partying and drinking at least half the nights of the week and was severely underweight. I weighed just under eight stone whilst standing at 5' 8". My bad relationship with food continued for years.

From the age of 13, I could not be single. I always had a boyfriend to try to fill the void I was feeling, to feel loved and wanted. I was extremely needy and as I got older, I chose men that on some level, I must have known would not be good for me. This went on until my early 20s. I kept getting what little confidence I had knocked down in this cycle of toxic relationships. Looking back, I must admit, I certainly had my part to play. I wasn't an easy partner or friend to have around. I was extremely negative about everything and would continue the same patterns and complaints over and over. Everyone spoke as if it were so easy to change, to have a positive mindset and to end a toxic relationship. This angered me because I felt it was impossible to change. Of course, now I know, it really is that easy. It's just about becoming self-aware. I've heard many times that it's all about perception, which is 100 per cent true. Is the glass half full or half empty? You decide. For me, at this point, the glass wasn't even half empty. There was no glass at all.

This is when the moment came, the definitive moment that changed the course of my life. I hit rock bottom. Now in hindsight, it would have been a lot easier to release my patterns of self-sabotage, my beliefs about the world and the people in it including myself, a lot sooner. I don't advise hitting rock bottom as it's a long climb back up. However, I obviously needed that big smack in the face.

So, there I was at the age of 23, alone in my flat. I was tired, exhausted and I had no idea who I was. I felt useless, unloved and worthless. I tried to call various family members because I knew I wasn't thinking straight. No answer. It was confirmed, no one would miss me if I was gone. So that was it. I decided life would be easier for others without me in it. I got out all the tablets I could find in the cupboard. Then bang, it hit me, I worked in complex care and was due to start a night shift just a few hours later. Wait, I did have a purpose, someone needed me. My job saved me.

I had a lot of time to think on a 12-hour night shift and that night, I decided that enough was enough. I couldn't carry on living this way and bringing everyone else around me down. I needed to change and perhaps it was about time I admitted what was really happening and to seek help. At the doctors' surgery, they weren't too keen on my choice to turn down anti-depressants. I was ready to peel back the layers and work on whatever was going on in my head, or so I thought. I had a rough start because I was carrying a lot of stuff, and I wasn't ready to accept full responsibility for where I was at. I was very good at passing the blame to everyone else. After a round of CBT (Cognitive Behaviour Therapy) to work on my beliefs, I felt a glimmer of hope. Was there a way out?

A friend then told me about a mindfulness group and asked if I'd like to give it a go with her. I literally had no idea it was meditation and found it all a bit odd and out there, but I persisted. My friend stopped attending and I continued. It felt like my weekly safe space where I could just let go and not be judged for just being me. At the group I was given the book *You Can Heal Your Life* by Louise Hay. I totally wasn't ready for that and after reading the first few chapters, I decided it was a load of rubbish. There was no way my life was in a mess because of me. Since then, I have read this book several times and I highly recommend it. I did start to find videos online and books that I was ready for and with these, I started my journey into personal development.

After my next relationship failed, that was it. I had been talking about travelling for a long time and I decided to do it. I had no idea how I was going to afford it and what I'd do when I came home. I don't think my work colleagues believed me at first because I'd been saying I was going to travel for the entire three years I'd been there. As the trip got closer, the fear was real. I owed thousands of pounds and I had no job to come home to. I had never even been on a holiday that wasn't with a boyfriend or family member. Now I was going to the other side of the planet. Luckily, I was going with a friend and I knew it would be an experience of a lifetime and I would work out what I wanted to do with my life. What an experience it was but I was wrong about the latter. I came home with still no clue what to do and where my life was going. From amazing adventures, conversations and challenges, I experienced a lot of growth. I still couldn't shake feeling lost and I just had this knowing there must be more to life. I wanted to feel a sense of purpose and fulfilment. I wanted to give back to the world, make an impact, and help others on a huge scale.

A year later, my answer to everything I was looking for came. It was an opportunity to create freedom in my life, do what my heart called and help others to grow and develop. It was also an opportunity to live life on my terms because I just couldn't work for someone else. I couldn't keep feeling empty, I needed purpose. I knew I didn't want someone dictating my time and income or telling me when I must work and when I could have a few weeks off during the year. I could, in time, give back on a big scale like I'd always imagined and help those who don't have the privilege of opportunity. This was my answer I'd been asking for and of course, when it was shown to me, I said no. That's right no. I laugh to myself now as I'd been literally praying for an opportunity to give me all of this and I outright turned it down.

I was working 12 to 18-hour shifts five or six days a week in security at this point. No way did I have the time, plus what would people say? I couldn't be that person anyway, I wouldn't even have a job in a few months so I couldn't afford to start anyway. These were the reasons I used to justify my decision. As the story goes, this decision, thank goodness, was only temporary. I am grateful that at this point in my life I'd experienced some level of personal growth. Even though I was still close minded, I realised my excuses were just that: excuses. I was scared to try something new. In fact, it was fear creating these justifications. The real reason was that I didn't feel I was worthy Who was I to change my life and the lives of others? What if it didn't work? I was scared both to fail and to succeed because I didn't feel I was good enough. Only looking back do I recognise this. The biggest fear of all was the opinions of others. It was two and a half years ago when I followed my gut feeling and jumped in.

Since this time, I have stretched my comfort zone and faced challenges and obstacles. My gosh, I'm so grateful for them. Without them, I cannot keep growing. Daily, I fill myself up by meditating, reading personal development books and listening to inspiring audios. I write affirmations (they were weird at first), I purposely feel a sense of gratitude. I am intentional about my day, therefore my life. Now I'm all about the 'woo woo' as I've naturally moved towards spirituality. I never would have thought that I could feel so on purpose, fulfilled, connected. I have an amazing relationship with my body and food. A year ago, I quit my job I wasn't happy in after building my business alongside as a plan B. Plus I have a decent man in my life, bonus! I respect myself enough to only allow the right people and circumstances into my life and I have found a balance to be able to help others whilst not being a people-pleaser. In addition, I stopped caring what others think – that one took a while.

My message to you, dear soul, is this: If opportunity comes knocking and something in you is excited by it, but there's hesitation, just say yes. You never know where it could lead, and you can always change your mind later. I've learnt now to always say yes, even to what scares me. This has been a life changer for me. Did you know, physiologically fear and excitement feel the same? Turn the fear to excitement and just go for whatever it is you feel called to do. Don't be afraid to do something outside of your comfort zone. The best things happen on the other side of fear. Do what sets your soul on fire. That thing you've always wanted to do, do it. If you're waiting for a sign, this is it.

You're not a tree so if you don't like where you are, move. Even in the darkest of times, I promise you there's always a way out, but it starts with you. There is so much light in this world. If you haven't found it yet, be the light for others so they can find you.

Small daily disciplined actions will lead to long-term change in the most profound ways.

Finally, remember this truth: You are worthy, you are enough and if you choose, you are limitless.

All my love, Charlotte.

LIVING THE LIFE I WANT

Zech Perry

Dear Reader,

It's Monday morning and the sun won't break the sky today. I've risen in darkness; I must work. But when was two days rest enough time for life? Withdrawn- becoming anxious – the rowdy mob- work day doubts- eyes on the mirror- self-conscious- time running out. Half-moons beneath the eyes add weight to my face. I'm about to start the list - all that is wrong - the hundredth count- How many new things do I possess? This could go on- the lists could go on- but no! Snap, and stop...

Mondays haven't always existed. They did during school days, but soon after they failed to make an appearance. A stretch of time I now use in all my work. The story is complex, and this is but a sketch.

Just after my completed youth, I found myself stitched in with a troupe of romantics. Swearing we'd live rather than serve, it became my counter experience to all I'd been told growing upwards. I was in love. A tribe of roamers sprawled hedonistically in each other's arms as the sun came up. For a while, it felt like the centre of the universe. Nothing was more important than the intricacies of our little society. Our bodies; our thoughts: clothes, books and words formed the basis of our hierarchy of promises, pacts and fluid unions. Contained within this circle, I operated well. I wasn't the greatest mouth, nor looked upon as base. I wasn't the funniest, but I certainly found my ideas most interesting- allowing myself great fleets of arrogance; it was the done thing.

Singing hymns to the wide-eyed night and dancing tenderly in to dawn was *just* fun. Bright and rebellious, I hadn't let the adult world derange my lust. Later, I would curse that ensemble, which I felt had betrayed the spirit- cheating the last kiss of youth.

There is a dawn out moment in my experience when I realised my band were greater performers than my innocent being could have known. Plying their brand of hedonism; selling their anarchy Thursday to Sunday. The in-between times spent hibernating safely inside the middleclass dream. Utilising the resources of wealth and social connection, they trained young shoots of ambition and brought far off personal adventures. Tendrils of their nepotistic webs assured their success, with minimal input.

Their disloyalty to the cause engendered a deep fracture within me. Change, why should anything change? If you had the world and all her material riches on strings, why would you choose a path whose destination was soulless conformity before rank old age? The betrayal was complete, and I was left the only romantic in my cosmos. For years, I harboured the cuts of an infant's loss. A black rot got in. A burnt seed- embryonic chaos set to flourish- sent for me to endure.

I've realised that I can't write about chaos and apathy as if it were some great pit I was thrown into. I was the pit and the boy who'd thrown himself in.

Time collapsed. I'd become so trapped that weeks openly bled into months and then years. My world had become a room- a dusty store of unread books and objects I'd found whilst in a state so detached, an ancient label became a book written whilst my finger traced the air. Plumes of incense had turned the ceiling black and the walls were jabbed with frenzied stabs of paint that slashed like knives during my tantrums and metaphorical attempts at escape. I'd developed a heavy dependence on alcohol, tobacco and imagination by this point. The last of which, I now understand kept me safe and stuck at the same time. As my slow withdrawal from society neared its completion, I conjured in to being vivid friends of the mind. I was an outcast, who'd successfully outcast himself. I was no longer the wondering romantic, nor the artistic boy with the pen in his hand.

Loneliness without insight or strength to embrace such a concept is the tap root of evil. I'd summoned my daemon: fear, anger and longing were his gifts, and physical sickness arrives when the mind is no longer able to keep it at bay. Imagination becomes delusion-coiled tight, ever burrowing towards the soul.

The bleeding of time continued, eight years passed unchanged bar a few meetings in which I attempted to cry for help.

I hear you say, "Why should I read on?" and "This morning is on a knife edge already" But you must - you must continue, so that you know the depths. If you glance at a dark place, you'll fly inside a sun laden sky thereafter!

Eventually my dirty book-space became a repository of empty cans and dead bottles topped up with human liquids. I kept the window open; always hoping some bird would fly in and befriend me. I took to the street often in search of an angel. But my figure had become known to local children who would call loudly to one another, "Look, it's him; how old is he? Tramp!" mistaking my once iconic velvet blazer- a poorly mended key to a lost time. During the bleeding of days, I wished up to the sky and down to the earth. I wished every strong man who passed was some knight in the process of realising his destiny. Riding in to my life, taking my hand and saving me from crying and cursing the moon.

Many precious objects were destroyed at that time. I look back at those things: a pocket watch, a sliver bird brooch and a blue glazed chalice all dashed against the wall.

There are two ways in which physical wounds may heal. The first is from the surface down into the bloody depths of the cut. The second is from the core to the surface. Secondary healing takes a lot longer and the wound seems open and dangerous for a while. I find this useful when thinking about the way I journeyed.

I'm certain of one thing dear reader and one thing alone. If any of this scrawl seems to promote a sense of lost hope, it shouldn't. The Goddess in the form of dreams and symbols decoded years later were the answered ravings posed to a bleak sky. Responses to my loneliness also came from another place- rippling in to my subconscious. The voice would say:

"This isn't the life you must lead; there's choice. There's a place of health beyond, a forest where life resides. Give yourself permission to find it"

Answers are obvious, but they're bold and uncomfortable. Answers rock worlds; they challenge self-pity, demanding you become the knight.

Hope, that hidden spirit, never lost, revealed itself. Every solution begins with hope. Spin your darkness around; let it bite its tail – the result is wisdom. Your pain and fracture are complex, but the solution can be traced back to the depths of your being. Three words to regain mastery of the self:

Hope- there will be change. Accept-things have happened. Forgive-what is done.

The daemon will transform and become your sword, your strength and your message. I have realised these are the bitterest panacea available. But take them with the sweet gold of your being, and all will be well.

I look at the Monday morning mirror; the half-moons under my eyes are hard won medals. I can sleep earlier at night, and not be dragged in to negative list making. Monday is the distance I've traversed on this journey. I know I'll always have a propensity for imagination as escape. I know I'll always feel a slave unless I'm living the life I want. I'm sure loneliness can't be the tap root of all evil, as loneliness teaches grace.

YWTMA, BB (Your Will Through Mine Always, Blessed Be)

Zechariah Perry

WAVE THE WHITE FLAG

Katie Oman

Dear Reader,

It's Monday morning and war has been declared...in my head at least.

Battle lines have been drawn, the troops are lining up and ready to charge, and the alarm clock only rang five minutes ago. On one side is the feared army known as You Suck. They're a terrifying mob of cutthroat bandits and outlaws, armed to the teeth and snarling as they wait to attack without mercy. The other side is a smaller unit, called Don't Be So Hard on Yourself. They may not have the same numbers as You Suck, but they're determined and ready to push through and come out victorious.

Why has my day started out this way?

I'm telling you, my life feels as though I'm the unwitting star of a movie that no one has ever told me about. Kind of like a cross between *Groundhog Day* and *The Truman Show*. Each weekday morning is as repetitive as the last, and Monday morning brings those feelings right to the surface that I'm about to get back on the merry-go-round.

Worse than that however is the unrelenting voice in my head that insists I'm a bad mum.

How could I not be?

All I seem to do is shout at my kids, stress myself into a complete frenzy and make each morning a battleground. If I'm not yelling at them to stop running around, then I'm shouting at them to hurry up. I must appear like some demented banshee, descending from her pit with the masses of wild hair and glowing eyes. I wouldn't be at all surprised if some big Hollywood producer didn't ring up later and ask me to be in his latest horror movie.

With a roar, the You Suck forces push forward, their weapons raised and ready to strike.

With a groan, I pull the duvet back over my head.

Why has it got to be such a battle each morning? Is it all my fault? Maybe if I was one of those naturally calm mums who gets up to do yoga and eat kale at 5am, then I'd be able to start the kids' day on a cloud of peace and Zen-like gracefulness. Or, maybe I'd be better just not caring so much. I could just tie up my hair in some scraggy ponytail, leave my onesie on, and not be too bothered if the kids are late for school or not.

But I can't be those things. I can only be me. The grumpy, impatient me.

You Suck rain blows down heavy onto Don't Be So Hard on Yourself, each one heavier than the last. The benevolent victims retreat, their forces dwindling by the vicious onslaught.

What if I scar them for life and they need endless therapy as they get older because of their mad mum? I can just picture them now, lying on some psychiatrist's couch while they weep of their crazy mum and her stress-filled ways.

I sigh deeply. I better get up and get my backside into gear if I'm going to earn enough money to pay for all that therapy; it won't come cheap.

My door softly pushes open, and my eldest son comes into my bedroom carrying a mug in his hands.

"Morning, mum. Thought I'd make you a cup of coffee. You okay?"'

I smile, the voices in my head quiet for a moment. *"Yes, thank you. Are you?"*

"Yeah, I'm good. Just getting my breakfast."

Handing me the mug, he leaves me alone once more and I look down at the steaming brown liquid. Maybe...just maybe...I'm not so bad. I mean, your son wouldn't just go and make you a coffee without being asked if you were the 'Worst Mum in the History of the World' now, would he?

The forces of You Suck are stunned as Don't Be So Hard on Yourself suddenly surge forward from nowhere; the unexpectedness of their retaliation catching them off guard. This wasn't supposed to happen. They'd been told to expect an easy victory on this Monday morning; same as it was every day.

Taking a deep gulp of coffee and feeling the burn slide down my throat, I heave myself out of bed to wake the twins. My heart is still heavy, despite the glimpse of hope on the horizon. Pushing open the door to their room, I take one deeper sigh and paint the friendly mum smile on my tired face.

"Morning."

"Good morning beautiful mummy!" A wave of love washes down from the top bunk of my bed as my daughter greets me in her normal exuberant tones. Feeling two small arms wrap around my waist, I look down to see my younger son hugging me tight. *"I love you mummy".*

Don't Be So Hard on Yourself troops swarm in, their numbers growing by the second. With a cry of dismay, the You Suck forces realise their defeat is imminent and fall back, waving the white flag as they go. They hadn't expected this back-up from the children; not today. And yet, here it was in all its glory. With that kind of support, there was no way they could have won this battle, not today. Seeing their surrender, the Don't Be So Hard on Yourself troops yelled out in thunderous celebration – a rare victory, but one that would hopefully set the foundations for less battles in the future.

Whatever tomorrow or the next day would bring, they knew that they had the means now to find their inner strength and come out the winner.

And that's what I want you to remember, today and every day. Sometimes it's tough to stop a vicious attack on yourself when you're in a space of self-hatred and judgement. The words we throw at ourselves can be unbelievably cruel. In this space, it can be hard to even know where to begin to turn things around. But, surround yourself with people that really love you- the good, bad, and ugly bits, and they will help you to come back to the thoughts that maybe you're not as bad as you're telling yourself you are. In fact, they will see you as damned wonderful and doing their best, no matter what. Being with them, no matter who they are, will help you to see this for yourself. Then, that nasty inner critic can go back into the shadows where it belongs.

Life can be tough enough at times. Don't let the nasty voices inside your head make it even harder for you than it needs to be.

REMEMBER

Kris Oster

Dear Reader,

It's Monday morning and someone is trying to reach me.

The heartbeat of the mother woke me up early, 4:44 am. The earth has her own rhythm and invites me to sync up with her. Subtle shivers like little tremors move through my body. It's electrical. My own inner alarm clock that reminds me that even on a dreary Monday morning, magic is afoot.

Sometimes it's 3:33 or 1:11. Or 2:22. Or 5:55.

It never fails. I wake up to repeating numbers almost every morning, and I believe there is someone reaching out to make contact.

Most of the time I suspect it is my mother who passed so quickly, and unexpectedly young at 67. I speak out loud, quietly, but audibly.

"Hi Mom. Anything I need to know today?"

Silence floats in the air like thunder clouds not quite willing to release the rain yet.

It's been nearly two years since she shifted beyond the veil.

"I miss you Mama."

More silence cradles me as I take a deep breath in to fill the empty space in my lungs. The grief has made a comfy home in that space.

This morning conversation of sorts is part of the repeating numbers game. I haven't quite figured out her code yet, but she's trying to remind me of something.

Remember ...

Remember what?

I pull out an oracle deck, her *Healing with The Angels* cards by Doreen Virtue. I like talking to her in the quiet mornings as if I'm talking to the earth herself. Her spirit is now a part of nature, and as long as I can remember, I've had lots of conversations with nature.

As I shuffle her cards and ask for her message, three babies fly out of the deck: "Friendship," "Dreams" and "Trust."

I lay all three on my altar and light a candle.

It's February 2nd, Imbolc after all (and made up of repeating numbers 2-2, no less).

Some call it Candlemas because it's a day to live, work and play by candle and fire light. The word *imbolc* translates as "in the belly." I feel pregnant with these messages and rather than rush to figure out the meaning I just sit in silence. A silence pregnant with possibilities and love.

Remember.

This other realm where my mom lives, with my grandmothers and grandfathers, loves lost, is alive and shimmering. I do not fear what happens after death. I've seen faery people and many a ghost. I saw my mother three or four times after she passed.

One of the final times I saw her was in her house. I saw her walk past my bedroom door, in the early morning hours of course. Back when I wasn't paying attention to the numbers on the clock, so I don't have a clue what the time was.

I followed her down the hallway and into her office. She stopped and was staring down at a drawer. She never looked at me. And shortly after this she evaporated into the air.

My stepfather heard me walking in the house and came out of his room.

"I just saw mom and she was looking at that drawer."

He bent down to inspect the drawer and found that it was filled with her diaries.

"I think she wants us to look in here and we will find a message from her."

He offered to go through the drawer of her random diaries, spiral notebooks and yellow legal pads. Her script was incredibly graceful and beautiful, like she was.

A few days later, he handed me a small box and said, "I think these were meant for you."

It took me a few days to look through these things. It has been difficult for me to say goodbye to my Rose. She wasn't just my mother, she was my best friend. Inside one of her notebooks was a letter she wrote me, never delivered. It was in the form of a poem about her love for me. I read it once. Maybe twice. Yet, still I keep it hidden in that box, inside the notebook.

I'm afraid to read it again, like something in me will crack.

I walk over to my altar where her ashes live inside a favourite jar she always admired at our local metaphysical store. After she died, I went back to buy it. It's a small Japanese raku pottery jar with a lid. It came with a tiny scroll of paper inside. The shopkeeper, Teresa, said it was a Dreamcatcher Jar.

I put mom's ashes in there and about a month or two later I pulled out the scroll and wrote my dreams and wishes so she would guard them for me.

I began to understand her messages. "Friendship." "Dreams." "Trust."

Maybe dreams aren't meant to be so guarded. Sometimes they feel too precious to let out in the open. Too tender for even my own eyes to read.

Remember.

Dreams are oracles and part of the natural world. They are flowy like water.

The great goddess of memory called Mnemosyne by the ancient Greeks was not just the mother of the nine Muses, she was also a river. Running right next to her was another river named Lethe, which means 'forgetfulness.'

I finally realized that my mom wants me to stay connected to my dreams, breathe them out into nature. Whisper my dreams into flowers, the grass, the trees, the air and of course the rivers, creeks and ocean.

When we become human-" doings" rather than human-" beings", we forget nature, the earth, our dreams. Forgetfulness is a strategy to avoid pain and suffering. We can function for sure, in that state. But how can we thrive in the river Lethe?

It is said that before a child's soul can be born it must first travel through the river Lethe, so it won't remember its past. It won't remember where it came from. Its sorrow and pain.

Mom wants me to release and surrender my dreams and trust that all will be OK. That it's OK to remember. Remember her. Remember her love and friendship that is all around me. All I need do is take a walk-in nature and I'm flooded with peaceful feelings.

If a dream, like water, is kept too long in captivity it will dry up. Dreams are meant to flow. They are meant to be shared freely.

I open my dream jar and read my scroll. I

fearfully look inside the box of her writings and photographs.

We keep those we love alive by remembering, as they recount in Mexican culture. *Día de los Muertos* celebrates remembrance every November 1st (not coincidentally, another holiday made of repeating numbers 11-1).

When we remember the dead, they continue to live on. But what does my mom want me to remember?

Her love for me.

When I went to look inside Mom's memory box, I found a letter that Saraphina, my daughter, wrote to me during her first week of kindergarten. My mom must have found it and put it somewhere safe, guarding it from being lost and forgotten.

My mom is important because she loves me. My favourite thing about my mom is she loves me. I love you! Love, Saraphina

Remember.

IT'S YOUR CHOICE

Lynn Meadowcroft

Dear Reader

It's Monday morning and I'm looking forward to the day ahead with love and joy! For I know that every day I have on this beautiful planet is a gift and I rejoice in the fact that this morning, I woke up.

Monday mornings didn't always feel like this. There was a time when I hated Monday mornings. For I knew that I had another whole week in front of me doing a job I didn't really like, working with people I had nothing in common with. Working for a boss who bullied me. Why would I look forward to Monday mornings?

My Monday morning mantra used to be, "It's Monday which means it's nearly Tuesday, which means it's nearly Wednesday, which means it's nearly Thursday, which means YEAH!!! It's nearly Friday!"

I used to live for Fridays. Monday through to Thursday had no meaning in my life. Friday meant it was the start of the weekend. Every Friday night I used to go out and get drunk, so drunk that most of the time I can't remember going home and I lived like this from 16 years old to 50 years old.

This was not living. This was running away from the pain I was in. This was running away from myself because the simple fact was, I didn't like who I was.

So, what happened to change my life?

I was on the verge of a nervous breakdown and had now become a single parent with two teenage sons when my sister gave me a book by Louise Hay called *The Power Is within You*. And when I read that book, I could not stop crying. Finally! I understood. It was me. I was the one who could change.

I had spent years trying to change everyone else because I believed it was all 'their' fault.

I was so passionate about the book and Louise Hay's philosophies that I wanted to share them with as many people as possible. So, I googled to see if there was any training and much to my delight, I discovered that there was a programme called, *Heal Your Life Teacher Training* once a year in the UK. So, I enrolled on the programme in 2011 and in 2012 I did the coaching training. In 2018 I also did the business training programme,

Managing with Heart and Mind.

Louise Hay's philosophy in a nutshell is, "It's only a thought and a thought can be changed."

Our thoughts lead to how we feel which in turn lead to our behaviour.

I discovered my limiting beliefs that had been affecting me my whole life and learnt that these beliefs had been something that I had learnt as a small child.

Some of my core beliefs were; "I am not good enough." "I am not deserving." "I am not worthy."

I had no idea I had these beliefs until I learnt about Louise Hay's philosophies.

I remember being told constantly at school, "You will never amount to anything." I remember at home being told constantly, "You don't deserve ...."

I remember as a child that I was always comparing myself to other children, believing that they were ' better' than me. That they were ' cleverer than me'. I remember the star chart we had with all the children's' names on and gold stars placed at the side of our names. I had about two or three stars and some other children had about 14 or 15 stars, which made me believe that I wasn't good enough. That there must be something wrong with me.

Of course, none of this was true. It was something that as a small child I had believed.

Hence, the life I had until being around 50 years old. I still believed I was not good enough, that is one of the main reasons I went out every Friday night and got so drunk.

I have now changed those old limiting beliefs to, "I am good enough." "I am deserving." "I am worthy."

I now understand that I create my own reality with the thoughts I have, which is why I no longer get up on Monday morning dreading the day and week ahead....no wonder I had such a bad time!

I now get up on Monday morning grateful to be alive! I look forward to the day ahead with love and joy and that makes me FEEL so good.

You see, when we are small children, we believe the people around us; parents, grandparents, aunties, uncles, teachers, church leaders to name a few.

I am not blaming parents or anyone else; they were doing the best they could with the knowledge and understanding they had at that time.

Yet the effect these childhood messages have is profound. And the thing is, that little girl/boy still exists within you. What you have not realized is that you are an adult now and you do not have to believe these childhood messages any more.

The key is to become aware of what these messages were that you believed in when you were growing up that still affect you today.

I can see very clearly now that because I had the belief that I was not good enough; that belief stopped me from doing many things. I did not apply for jobs because I believed I would not get them because I was not good enough. I played 'small' believing that I was 'nobody' so why would people listen to me? So, I chose not to have a voice. I followed the crowd. I became a people-pleaser. I wanted people to like me, dare I be bold enough to say I wanted people to love me. I sought the approval of others. So, I said yes to everything even when it meant compromising my own happiness.

After my marriage ended, I was in another relationship in which I put his needs above my own. In which I put him before my own children. In which I accepted his mental abuse daily. In which I absolutely felt unloved, unattractive, and like I did not deserve better.

That relationship ended after seven years of me being mentally abused almost every day. In which I cried myself to sleep most nights. In which, once again, I believed that I was a failure. That there was something wrong with me. That I wasn't good enough.

It was only when I began to learn to love myself that I felt stronger. I began to like who I was. I was doing my mirror work daily (this is a concept advocated by Louise Hay, where you look in the mirror every day, into your own eyes and say, "I love you Lynn. I love and approve of you." You then add anything else you might want to say.) Mirror work is very powerful. It is not about being vain. It is about you connecting deep within with that little girl and feeling the power of love for yourself and your little girl.

When I look back on how my life used to

be, I see all the ways I did not love myself.

I am not blaming myself or criticising myself here. I have done that for years and all that did was make me feel shit about myself.

I see how the thoughts and beliefs I had about myself and others and the world led me to feel anxious, worried, depressed and unhappy.

So much has changed, and I am so very happy now. I know I have the power within me to create my own reality with the thoughts I have so I am very mindful of the thoughts I now choose.

I also connect with my inner child every day. I tell her how much I love her. I tell her how precious she is. I tell her how special she is. I tell her all the things I wanted to hear when I was a small child.

I understand she is part of me, and I also understand that I am an adult now and so it's up to me to make wise, adult choices.

My invitation to everyone reading this is to let go of being a victim. It does not serve you. It keeps you stuck. Stop telling your story about how bad your life is and how unfair life has been to you.

That is exactly how I used to think.

Instead, embrace who you are. Know that who you are is good enough. Know that you deserve to have a wonderful life full of love, joy and peace. Know that you are worth loving. Know that you are magnificent.

I invite you to stand in your own power. Stop giving it away to others. Be the magnificent woman/man you were born to be.

Start living your life.

Think better thinking thoughts which will create better feelings which will lead to better actions.

It is all up to you. What is it that you really want? Pain and suffering or joy and freedom?

I made my choice and I am living the life of my dreams.

What choice will you make?

Maybe after reading this you will now say, "It's Monday morning and I feel so grateful to be alive!"

A CARING LAD CHANGED MY LIFE

Ben Hornsby

Dear Reader,

It's Monday morning and I'm in my flat, overlooking Portsmouth train station, thinking to myself that I have had many worse Monday mornings. In fact, every day of the week was pure misery.

Let's rewind back to when I was 11-years-old and sexually abused by four, older female friends. I was drunk that day. I found myself semi-naked in a wood near my home in Oxfordshire. I don't know how I got to those woods but when I sobered up, I found my friends taking turns to perform sex acts on me. I was completely embarrassed by being seen that way. I spent the rest of my teenage years trying to be a man because I felt as if the girls who had done this to me would see me as a child (even though I was a child). At that time, my idea of being a man was to misbehave, cause crime, drink and take drugs. From the ages of eleven to sixteen, that's exactly what I did. I experimented with all the street drugs because it was a way of escaping the thoughts that went through my mind. I was always an anxious, nervous, shy child anyway but the more drugs I took, the less anxious and worried I became.

I came across heroin when I was sixteen. There's not much I can say about my life back then apart from it went in a continual decline. I became severely addicted and I thought I couldn't stop. I used heroin from the age of 16 until I was 34, mainly injecting it. During those years, I was in police custody quite regularly for shoplifting, burglary and drug dealing. I have 50 convictions. I've been to prison on two occasions and on the second time, I was handed a three-and-a-half-year sentence for selling heroin to undercover police officers. You would have thought I would have learnt my lesson and stopped taking drugs, but I never did. When I was released from prison, the first thing I did was walk into a pub and then a week later, I was back to being addicted to heroin.

I never understood the power of addiction until I ended up in rehab. Before rehab I hit the rock bottom of homelessness and street begging. I really did hate myself for how I had become, and I wanted to die. I became suicidal and reckless, I didn't care anymore. I overdosed but fortunately somebody called an ambulance and they brought back to life with a jab of adrenaline to the spine, I do believe.

One day, I experienced a shift in the way I felt about myself. I was begging outside a shop in Banbury, Oxfordshire when a little boy came over to me and gave me a bottle of water and £3 from his pocket. He was only about eight-years-old, and his kindness broke my heart. There was no way I would have done that at his age, and I started thinking that if he feels sorry for me then why couldn't I feel the same way towards myself? I picked my sorry arse off the floor and decided that I couldn't do it anymore. I sought help from a drug drop-in centre called Turning Point and they got me funding for rehab.

I spent nine months in rehab at the Arc in Portsmouth. While there, they brainwashed me into believing in myself and knowing anything is possible. I learnt to love myself again and I learnt how to change and control my thinking. I changed all my old negative beliefs about myself into positive ones, I started stepping out my comfort zone by embracing my anxiety head on. For once, anxiety didn't control my life and I had control of my life through my thoughts. I went in that rehab centre broken but I came out as a new man on a mission to achieve as much as I possibly could while I still had the chance.

I never thought I would see the boy who helped me again. On the first of January

2018, I put a post on social media asking people to help me find him and two weeks later, the boy's mum got in touch with me. National newspapers had seen my social media post and they got involved in the hunt. I ended up featured in the Daily Star and Daily Mail. I finally got to meet the boy again on the Jeremy Kyle TV show. Initially, I turned down the offer but when they rang me to explain I would be on an inspirational story episode being aired on Mother's Day, I decided to go ahead. I'm very glad I did because the boy, Emmanuel, was given lots of treats including a holiday for him and his mum.

I made a promise to myself to help as many people as I could because I couldn't think of any other way of paying Emmanuel back for his kindness.

I've spent the last three years helping people. I set up a Facebook group called 'Feel the fear and embrace your true self'. People reach out to me through the Facebook group for many reasons but mainly it's because they want a better life. Because of this, I've decided to become a life coach and my big dream is to be a motivational speaker. I've had the opportunity to do some talks, so my dream is slowly manifesting itself into reality. It's a far cry from the homeless, suicidal heroin addict who hated himself.

I now love life. I learnt to be in control of my thoughts. I can't complain about my life now because I know anything is possible if you put your mind to it.

It's funny now because Monday is my favourite day. Every day is as good as the other and if you think Mondays are shit then I'm sorry to tell you Monday is not shit, your thinking is.

LIFE IS PRETTY GOOD AFTER ALL

Joy Andreasen

Dear Reader,

It's Monday morning and that 6am alarm just jolted you out of your happy place under your down alternative comforter and reminded you that the sun in fact, does come out again no matter whether you are ready for it or not.

Monday mornings remind me that no matter whether the weekend held fun filled hanging out with friends, perhaps an impromptu excursion to the beach, or a couple days of catching up with all the chores you didn't have time to do during the week, every day is, in fact, a new beginning and another chance to reinvent your version of yourself.

So many times, we dread that Monday morning alarm. We drag ourselves out of bed and mutter to ourselves that we really didn't sign up for this.

I remember when I was young, I envisioned myself a famous artist, or even a preacher's wife. Not in my wildest imaginations did I see myself getting up and going to a regular 9 to 5 job day in and day out for the entirety of my life, just like my mother did before me.

But life happened. I married young without too much thought on choosing the right partner. My self-esteem convinced me that I may not get another offer, so I jumped on the first one that stuck around for more than a month. Before you know it, I had a child and a husband who regarded work as an inconvenience and an interference into his playtime. To avoid raising my child in a car, I secured a job that paid well and offered health insurance.

But my soul always longed for more.

Years and years went by. I frequently complained to one of my co-workers about the louse I'd married and his inability to keep a job. One day, that co-worker surprised me with a challenge.

He told me to stop complaining about my lot in life and do something about it. He remarked that if I was unwilling to make that change, then stop complaining to him because he wasn't going to listen anymore. Tough words.

Up until then, I was convinced that if I prayed long and hard enough, Jesus himself would come down from heaven and either strike my husband dead or miraculously transform him into a man of character and responsibility.

Neither one of those things happened.

The day I realized that my life was up to me was the day I stopped praying for some outside Force, be it Jesus or Someone Else to fix my life.

I guess in a way it wasn't completely my fault. How many fairy tales are we told as little girls that promise us a knight in shining armour who comes in and saves the day. Couple that with my strict church upbringing, I'd combined the two into thinking that Jesus was the knight in shining armour and, you get the rest of the story.

Unfortunately, Jesus stood me up. That one fateful day when my co-worker alerted me to the fact that if I wasn't happy, it was my responsibility to change it, completely shattered my world. Jesus and my belief in the knight in shining armour all came crumbling down like the three little pigs and their houses, with one puff of wind from the not so big bad wolf.

It wasn't easy. I walked out of the house and my marriage with five changes of clothes and a hairdryer.

Sometimes you must completely lose everything to find yourself.

If you find yourself in a position where life

seems unfair, where perhaps another person seems to be holding you back from being your best self, or perhaps you are weighed down with debt or a debilitating illness, take it from me that there is no obstacle that can keep you down if you decide to overcome it.

Our best advocate is our belief in ourselves and our own awesomeness!

It has been many years since the day I walked out of my home of 18- years with only a few changes of clothes. The day I walked out, I knew that one day I'd have everything I lost back, only better. I was forced to declare bankruptcy and file for divorce as one of those bundle deals. It was truly a starting over.

Fate wasn't done with me. Somehow in those years of feeling lost, alone and powerless, I had forgotten an ability to speak with Spirit. When I remembered, once again I was faced with that demon of self- doubt. Every time someone came to me for a message from the Spirit world, I would wring my hands and worry. What if the dead don't show up? What if their Angels have nothing to say, or worse, what if they do but I can't hear them?

In the beginning I only delivered messages to close friends, family members or people who were referred to me. One day, one of my customers at the Post Office where I worked had decided to come and see if her brother would come through and tell her the truth about how he died. I was beside myself with worry. What if he doesn't tell me?

Once again, my Spirit people reminded me

of my awesomeness. They told me that all day long before she came, I was to declare that I was an amazing medium and heard the voice of the spirit world with ease.

Needless to say, her brother came through with the information she requested.

No matter what the circumstances that seem to hold you hostage, you can overcome!

Recently my (current) husband gave me a present of a very detailed and intricate drawing done by a woman who creates art with her teeth since she has no hands. I watched a news piece just the other day about a man who is totally blind but makes his living as an architect. One of his accomplishments is creating a public transit system that is blind friendly by changing the texture of the concrete on which they walk! How can we even think that the struggles we deal with day to day even come close to the obstacles these two individuals have overcome?

I find that when I am in a dark place, doubting my worth and feeling sorry for myself (and, yes, it happens), I tend to energetically repel clients. No one is calling me for readings or signing up for classes. But when I shake it off and tell myself that I am awesome and everyone knows it, people are finding me from websites that I don't even advertise on.

Just for today, tell yourself you're awesome. You have gifts and abilities that are unique to you. You're a money magnet. You're blessed with abundant health, happiness, joy and loving relationships. Good things are always happening to you. Every time you turn around, something wonderful happens.

The more joy we invite into our lives, the higher our energetic frequency. In other words, the happier we are, the more we attract wonderful things into our lives. Law of attraction? Yes!

I can't guarantee that if you are in a wheelchair you will walk again, or if you are in jail, suddenly you will be released. I can guarantee that miracles will happen that will allow you to flourish no matter where you are or what challenges face you.

This Monday morning, instead of dreading another work week at a job you despise, thank your Soul and whatever you consider to be your Higher Guidance System that you have a life that is blessing you with everything you need and some or most of what you want. Expect unexpected blessings to hunt you down and life to be one joyous moment after another.

One day you'll realize that life is pretty good after all.

WHAT GIVES YOU JOY?

Melinda Annear

Dear Reader,

It's Monday morning and I wonder how you feel? Right this second. Peaceful, tired, anxious, happy, worried, content, bored, excited, dread? What about joy? What gives you joy?

This isn't a question I'd ever heard before, until after I finished studying to be a kinesiologist.

I had a moment where I felt very tired and low, so I went to the doctor explaining I didn't feel right. I described my symptoms and she said, "You're depressed, you need anti-depressants." Thanks, but no thanks, I know what depression feels like and it wasn't this. I contacted my kinesiology teacher for advice.

She kindly drove over to give me a session, in which she discovered I needed Omega 3 and I felt back to normal after a month.

What was interesting was that she asked me what gave me joy "Sorry?" I said, so she repeated: "What gives you joy?" For some reason, it threw me off guard because I'd never thought to ask myself that question. I responded eventually, "My dog" then quickly added "and my husband of course" (I know what you're thinking but his [the dog's] cuteness is unbelievable and by far outweighs my husband's).

Then a couple of years ago, this question popped up again. My mother and I went to a psychic circle to see if we had any gifts we could unearth. Before anything took place, the organiser protected the space and began with a guided meditation. She asked us to open our hearts and to think about what gave us joy. Afterwards, my mother admitted it gave her pause for thought. Eventually she thought of my dog. I told you he was cute.

Now don't believe for a second that my dog is the only thing in life that gives my mother and I joy. However, I do believe this is a question that is rarely asked of ourselves or of others, which is why it can make us pause for a moment. Outside of the obvious such as children, family, animals and our partners, surely, we should know this in an instant.

In my formative years, my life was full of joy. I was a tomboy that loved climbing trees, digging clay out of the back garden, and building dens. So, when we moved to Scotland for two years, it was heaven for me. Our back garden was practically vertical with huge rocks embedded into it, a purpose-built climbing frame. In the winter, the playground would freeze in large vertical lines, so everyone would take it in turns to run and slide down the ice every break time. At weekends, we would go on family walks in the most stunning countryside, passing breath-taking lochs and mysterious forests. Life was good.

Then it was time to move back to Hampshire, aged about nine, into a new junior school and straight onto the film set of *Mean Girls*. In Scotland, if someone didn't like you, they made it clear. They were direct with their feelings, admittedly with the odd Chinese burn on the wrist thrown in for good measure, but we all knew where we stood, and the playground dynamic ran smoothly.

However, it was extremely confusing in the sunny south. To begin with, they were all shiny and smiling, enticing you into their friendly group. Then the ring leader would be giggling about you behind your back, then telling you that they liked you best, while encouraging the rest of the group to say horrible things to you.

I wasn't qualified for this kind of emotional warfare, it was so confusing and upsetting; perhaps they had experienced this from older sisters? However, I was a tom-boy with an older brother, we sorted disputes through wrestling, and I'd mastered the Chinese burn to perfection. Punch me in the face any time of the day rather than the hurtful sting of their words, normally about my weight (despite being a skinny nine-year-old) and my hair (afro hair was rare in my small town). This bizarre 'friendship' full of fun, undermining, love, dread, loyalty, and anxiety continued until I was 16 with this particular 'Mean Girl'.

During this time, when I was 14, my grandmother was diagnosed with terminal ovarian cancer and she chose to spend her last remaining months living with us. There's only so much you can do to help when you're 14 and as she got worse, I hit the biscuit tin. The weight piled on, while ironically, I developed an interest in fashion, constantly drawing designs and immersing myself in the pages of beautiful slim models in beautiful clothes. Their lives looked so perfect.

Then I had a light bulb moment. If I was slim again, no wait, even better, skinny, then everything would be fine. This is how I would manage all this pain. I'd found a new friend called an eating disorder, who told me I would feel better about everything if I was skinny. It made perfect sense.

So, my new friend and I continued to hang out for another 20 years, even though I'd realised some time ago that this one wasn't good for me either. Somehow, I'd become stuck in this relationship, and I didn't know how to get out of what was becoming a very dark place. Another twisted friendship that was even harder to end.

I moved to London to study then began employment in well paid jobs that left me feeling stressed or numb. All the recreational activities that go with them left me drained and exhausted. However, I'd found a group of kind, fun, normal friends that weren't mean, but due to my insecurities and trust issues, it took a while for me to acclimatise with the females of the group. But, I'm happy to report that most of them stuck by me through my wobbly times, unaware of my eating disorder, of which I was deeply ashamed. Some are still my friends to this day.

I continued to share my warped thoughts with different therapists, ending up as an outpatient in an eating disorder unit in London. During all this 'quality' time with my eating disorder, it promised it would keep me safe from my feelings and past pains. That it wouldn't let me down, I would be in control and no-one could hurt me if we stayed friends. My earth angel mother tirelessly tried to separate us through numerous alternative and complimentary therapies. She was the reason I started to believe I could break free from this eating disorder.

Then something amazing happened. My mother encouraged me to do a healing course with her. I wasn't sure what to expect and I was a little nervous. When the meditation and attunement took place, I was overwhelmed by such peace, a sense of coming home and such love that sent me into a blubbering mess. The healing my soul had been crying out for had arrived, I was filled with an unconditional love, I was filled with joy!

At my next appointment at the eating disorder unit I told my psychotherapist I didn't need to come anymore, and she agreed. She was amazed at the speed of my progress and asked me what had led to my transformation. So, I told her about the healing, expecting her to scoff at my response. Surprisingly she responded that she believed in it too but wasn't allowed to recommend such modalities to her patients.

A few years later, my father was diagnosed with prostate cancer and I felt as though my world had caved in. Memories of my grandmother's illness came flooding to the forefront, but my doctor assured me this particular cancer could be controlled. However, despite this reassurance, I couldn't control the inner anxiety and dread.

The difficulty of experiencing a previous trauma is that the brain remembers how your thoughts and body responded at that time. When facing a situation that reminds the brain of the past trauma, it will respond with the same level of intensity, even if it isn't appropriate to the current situation. It's a built-in survival technique.

So, despite the reassurance from my doctor, I was a mess at times, because my brain's instinctive response was that my father would end up the same way as my grandmother. However, this time I felt all the raw pain in its glory, past and present. Then I let it go, instead of burying it in starvation or purging, alcohol, anti-depressants, the list goes on. I'd made peace with my pain.

After being in London for 17 years I moved back home to be closer to my parents to offer support through this new journey. I reconnected with some dear old friends that were not associated with the mean girl circuit and I felt saddened with the friend choices when I was younger. Thankfully, they are my close trusted friends to this day. I also met my husband at a school reunion, we bought a house together two years later and I accepted a new job commuting to Brighton. Things were looking up.

I'd been in my new job for nine weeks setting up a new sector, when I found out I was nine weeks pregnant. I was in shock. No maternity leave and commuting four hours a day. How was I going to have this baby?

Once I was over the initial shock, I was now getting excited about this little life growing inside of me. Three days before my 12-week scan, I treated myself to my first maternity dress for a wedding that was coming up. As soon as I got home from the shops, I tried on my new dress. While I admired my little bump in the mirror, I started to bleed. Over the phone, I was told to expect the worst, and it was the worst. That weekend, I went through two days of unbelievable physical and emotional pain. Eight weeks later, I lost my job along with my sense of self and my purpose.

I was broken and eventually financially broke. I was later diagnosed with Generalised Anxiety Disorder and PTSD.

Subsequently, I stopped getting dressed, getting up and leaving the house. My husband became very concerned and encouraged me to find a part-time job to build my confidence. Eventually, I found a part-time job and I began rebuilding myself through meditation. I then found the confidence to start my own business as a massage and beauty therapist, which I'd previously trained for. Six months later, we lost another baby in the early stages. Thankfully, I'd begun CBT to deal with the first miscarriage.

While having some spiritual counselling with my meditation teacher, she suggested looking into kinesiology. I went to a taster teaching session and I knew immediately this was my calling. Everything I'd experienced and learned had led me to this, this was my purpose, this was my joy. It was also my saviour. It enabled me to release all past emotional pain held in my body and heal the damage I'd inflicted on my body. My hormones were out of balance, my digestion was non-existent, so I was sensitive to every food, I was constipated from my grief – the list went on. Thankfully, kinesiology healed my mind, body and soul.

Do I wish my grandmother passed away in a hospital instead? Absolutely not, the joy we all experienced being together as a family was worth it all and she just laughed and laughed her way to the other side. I have such wonderful memories held in my heart. I also learnt the power of emotional pain, the physical impact and the different ways we try to avoid it, when really, we should face it, embrace it and release it. There's always a light shining in the darkness, you just must look for it.

My father is still going strong, 10 years since his diagnosis and we have become closer than ever, something that would not have happened if I had stayed in London. And of course, I wouldn't have met my best friend, my rock, my true love, my wonderful husband.

The miscarriages still bring me sadness, even now as I write this, my heart aches, but my fur baby Archie always brings back my joy. Throughout this pain, my husband and I have built an unbreakable bond by going through something so traumatic, our marriage is stronger than ever.

I could still be in the rat race, but my trauma led me to my purpose, on to the path of kinesiology to help others release their pain.

I gratefully embrace every emotional and physical experience that I've been through as it has made me who I am. Those experiences have enabled me to help others overcome their obstacles on their journeys. However, I've also learnt that every emotion and thought you have, your body listens closely and believes everything. Be mindful of your thoughts, be mindful of who you surround yourself with, and ask for help when you are in that dark place. Be mindful of what gives you joy. I wish the younger me knew to ask herself what gave her joy and discarded situations or people who didn't.

Please know dear reader, that my life has not been all doom and gloom, I've had the most amazing and joyful adventures. I've chosen to share some of my pains with you, to encourage you to look for the light in your darkness and to ask yourself what gives you joy?

My parents bought me a book called *Spark Joy, an illustrated guide to the Japanese Art of Tidying* by Marie Kondo. Kondo's motto is as you clear your home, hold each item and ask yourself does it spark joy? If not, thank it then discard it.

Imagine if we asked ourselves this question in relation to everything in our lives? Our job, our friends, our partners, our home, everything. Isn't it the ultimate act of self-love to ask what sparks joy in our lives and to immerse ourselves in that joy? And those things and people that no longer spark joy, is it time to say thank you for everything then let them go? People, jobs, material items are not always right for us forever, because we evolve, our tastes and interests change.

Find the joy within you. Find the light in the darkness. Find what makes your heart sing. Fill your surroundings, your time, your efforts with only those that give your joy. Let that be your quest in this lifetime.

So dear reader, I ask you again, "What gives you joy?"

MY HIDDEN CHILDREN

F.A.W.

Dear Reader,

It's Monday morning and the last few weeks have been hard.

You see, my story really started 43 years ago, but I've only been aware of it for just over six years. Because, in December 2012, I found my forgotten children. My inside children I'd buried for 25 years.

Why did they surface in 2012? Well, part of it was that I should have been the happiest I'd ever been. I had everything I'd ever wanted. I had a wife, we'd been together for nine years and our family had grown with our many four-legged children. My partner and I were both in managerial positions. We had just bought a brand-new car, which was something I'd always dreamed of doing and we were in the process of buying our first house. However, in September 2012, I'd started to dance with the black dog of depression.

It wasn't a new dance, it was one I'd been well used to since childhood but in the nine years since I'd met my partner, I'd forgotten the steps. We'd had some rough times, as people do. My partner was suffering from chronic pain, which no one (not even the specialists) seemed able to sort out. I'd been bullied by my previous manager, had finally spoken up, and then became part of a management team of which one of the three was also a bully.

I knew I had a lot to be happy about, and yet I was struggling with low self-esteem and depression. I went to the doctor to see about anti-depressants, and whilst she did prescribe them, she also recommended cognitive behavioural therapy (CBT). I was scared by the idea of this because it seemed I would have to look at my childhood. I was aware that my mum had struggled with depression when I was a child, and that she had been what most people would class as emotionally abusive. I was also aware that I had no memories of my childhood, and that generally if this happened it was because of trauma. However, I wanted to shake off the depression, so I was willing to try.

Bizarrely, my first memory appeared before the CBT started, and it was all down to Jimmy Saville.

I was reading a newspaper article about the

accusations surrounding Jimmy Saville perpetrating childhood sexual abuse in the 70s and 80s when the room I was in faded away and I found myself in the kitchen of my childhood home, laying on the floor with my parents examining my privates. They were doing this because I was sore there. I remembered that mum had made dad take me to the doctor. In this memory, I was around four-years-old, and I knew the reason I'd been sore there was because dad had been sexually abusing me since I was a baby.

My world crashed in. I immediately knew this was why I didn't remember my childhood, good or bad. My mind had blocked everything, because if I remembered anything good, I might also remember the bad.

So, what did this mean? I had hated my dad in my teens – I remembered that, and I'd often struggled with the way mum was. However, I did love them, and I found it hard to reconcile the dad I'd learned to love with someone who would sexually abuse a child. Mum had sent him to the doctor with me, when she always took us herself, so had she known? I couldn't talk about this to my partner, because if this were true, and she knew, would she hate my parents? Did I hate them? No, I couldn't. I must have done something to make him behave like that. And if that were true, would my partner hate me if she knew? I told my CBT counsellor on our first session, and she said this wasn't something we could explore. Not surprisingly, after that, I hid a lot of how I felt, and the CBT didn't work. But it was eating me up inside and I started wanting to self-harm, to cut the pain out. I found a support group online and stayed up late into the night chatting. My partner and I struggled because of it.

Finally, I told her what I'd remembered. She said she'd support any decisions I made about my parents. She reminded me that once, several years before, midway through sex, I'd sat up in tears saying that Dad had sexually abused me. I had no recollection of this. I'd cried it out, then blocked it out again.

Over the next couple of years, I had more and more flashbacks of abuse. I knew he had touched me from as early as I could remember (still in nappies). At four (after the day he took me to the doctor) he started penetrating me with a finger. At seven he got me to masturbate him. It went on until I was 12.

My parents lived about 70 miles away from us, but we continued to see them every six weeks or so. I was struggling with this, but mum always made me feel guilty if it was any longer. I would tend to doubt whether the memories were true whenever I saw my parents, but between times I would start to believe myself again, only to ping back to disbelief when I saw them next. I found a counsellor, and she believed me.

We moved into our new house, and we now lived about 150 miles away from them, but still mum would insist on seeing us regularly. By this time, I'd also remembered that dad had raped me from the age of eight until I was 12, and that he'd stopped when my breasts grew because "dads couldn't love their daughter in the same way when they grew up".

After an 18 month wait, I was offered counselling at a local abuse and rape counselling service. After the first few sessions, I believed myself enough that I wanted to break contact with my parents. A month before my 40th birthday, I wrote to them and told them I had remembered dad being inappropriate when I was younger, and that I needed space to process it. They denied it. I told my brother, who was upset. He doesn't remember our childhood either, but he doesn't think he was abused. He supports me, and our parents.

Since breaking contact, I've remembered more and more. When I was six, I told a neighbour who confronted them. They said I was lying, then he punished me by washing my mouth out – with his sperm. On my seventh birthday he gave me the 'gift' of giving me oral sex, and once at 14 he sodomised me. The rapes happened 2-3 times a week, from eight-years-old to 12. That means somewhere between 416 and 624 times.

Over the past three-and-a-half years, I've had lots of counselling. In my head, rationally, I understand that he's a bad man, who did bad things, but still I rarely feel angry.

I can talk about this. I belong to a choir and we recently did a concert in aid of a local charity I attend which helps incest survivors. I spoke at the concert about my experiences to an audience of nearly 140 people. People congratulated me, called me brave. But that's the adult me. On my journey I've found that inside of me I have a sad four-year-old, a devastated and terrified six-year-old, a confused seven-year-old, a grieving eight-year-old, a lonely and empty twelve to seventeen-year-old, an angry fourteen-year-old, an adult that coped from seventeen to forty-two, and me.

I'm generally in the driving seat, but sometimes one of the 'littles' takes over emotionally, and I forget how to cope.

As adult me, I understand that I'm amazing. I've survived so much. I have four tattoos that I've had done specifically to remind me of this when I struggle. The first one is a big koi. Koi tattoos symbolise struggle. If it is swimming up, it shows an ongoing struggle, swimming down denotes a struggle overcome. Mine is swimming up and is coloured the green that is used for the depression awareness ribbon. I have the words 'believe in yourself' and 'you are amazing' tattooed. And I have a butterfly made up of support ribbons. Its body is a lime green ribbon, for childhood sexual abuse. Its wings are made up of ribbons in green (for depression), purple (for sexual or domestic abuse) and teal (for childhood abuse and anxiety awareness). This is because depression and anxiety will forever be part of my life due to the abuse. Following the lines of the butterfly's body it reads: CSA survivor (CSA = childhood sexual abuse).

In 2018, I reported my father to the police.

They're investigating. If they can find enough evidence, it will go to court.

If people will listen, I will speak out. For one reason, my innocent inner children need to be heard. For another, the more survivors speak out, the more awareness grows, and the more difficult it becomes for perpetrators. And finally, if I can make just one survivor feel less alone, I feel I will have done my job.

I'm slowly writing my complete story into a book, warts and all, in the hopes to make this hellacious healing journey a little easier for some. Or to allow a non-survivor a new insight into the world of a healing survivor because we never know who we might meet on our journey.

I've come such a long way on my journey, but I still have a long way to go. I need to learn how to nurture and comfort my inner children, so they feel safe. Recently my partner and I converted our civil partnership to a marriage. I chose to leave my father's details off the marriage certificate. A freeing choice but one that has also sparked my grieving eight-year-old with the realisation that my daddy is someone of whom I'm ashamed, someone whom I want to deny.

I struggle often with thoughts of self-harm, and suicide.

And yet, despite this, here I stand on this Monday morning. Air in my lungs, on a bright new day. I still have my wife, and the family I CHOOSE. We have our house, which is filled with a variety of pets. We have my wife's family, and my brother and his family. And despite still having major anxiety and some depression, I have a job I enjoy. We have a car, and the means to fill it, and we have the means to feed and clothe ourselves. I have a few friends who support me, and for whom I'm grateful. I have two support groups I attend, and a few online support groups too. I'm soon to embark on more counselling by a specialised charity.

So, life is tough but despite everything, I still get to be incredibly thankful that when things are at their worst, and I consider the temptation to step off the ride of life, I have too many things that keep me here. I can still love. I can still see the beauty of the world around me. I still have people who care for me. I surround myself with other survivors, and with people who love life. I'm slowly learning that I matter. That I'm worthy. I've shed abusive relationships and filled my life with people who hold each other up. When one of us is struggling, there's usually one of us saying something that reminds us of the beauty in life. I have enough blessings to count that will keep me moving on, healing, and hoping to help others.

THE SPACE BETWEEN WANT AND NEED

Luke Voulgarakis

Dear Reader,

It's Monday morning and I can't open the door. It was what seemed to be an average morning at the start of my working week back in 2011, except this morning turned out to be anything but average. As I awoke at 7:15am to the shriek sound of my Tazmanian Devil alarm clock (yes, you read that right), I began my usual three snoozes before finally emerging from my cosy nest at 7:30am. I showered, brushed my teeth, dressed and headed for the front door. As I reached for the shiny, brushed chrome lever, something washed through me. A shudder of fear, self-doubt and overwhelm cast its shadow upon me. There was nothing physically wrong with that door handle, nor was there anything physically wrong with my ability to operate it. Yet, there in front of me, was an impossible challenge. This shadow that lurked over my shoulder completely impaired my motor skills. I was left utterly helpless to perform the simplest of tasks, a task that I'd performed thousands of times before. But how could this be? And why was it happening to me? Things like this don't happen to me.

I rushed to the phone and diligently called my workplace without a thought as to how I was going to explain myself. When my call was answered, I opened my mouth to speak and no words came out. Instead, a garbled mash of nonsensical hysterics escaped my mouth. I eventually managed to choke my name out before sobbing uncontrollably until I hung up. What had just happened? I am not an emotional person.

For four months following this, I was unable to return to the workplace. Stress had gotten me, shaken me, beaten me and left me for dead. I was out for the count.

Fast forward eight years, and here I am, sharing my story, living the life of my dreams, and thanking every god, angel, star and lucky unicorn (or whatever you believe in) for that fateful Monday morning because it was the catalyst for my greatest life story thus far.

My journey over this time has taken some peaks and troughs. Once I eventually returned to the workplace, I was immediately struck with fear again, realising that I'd lost a portion of my memory from the weeks leading up to my break-down. To experience a loss of memory that wasn't self-induced by narcotics was an incredibly frightening moment for me, a moment that will never leave me. It was in this instant that I made the decision to move on from this workplace. Now you might think that this was an obvious decision regardless of the memory loss but, for me, I'd worked my whole life to be in this role, for this company. It was everything I'd dreamed of, and while I was only 26 at the time, I'd wanted this since I was 14 years old. I'd geared my education, my work experience, my life around getting myself into this position. So, to let go was a far greater deal than anyone could have imagined. I had failed.

Over the next seven years, I hopped from job to job, really struggling to settle into anything that felt meaningful. I pined for my previous role because I'd put so much of myself into it. But to what avail? What did I achieve from giving it everything I had? My job defined me, but my job broke me. So now what? I had no identity, I was still broken and scarred, and even worse, I was totally lost in myself. I felt utterly hopeless.

This caused me to question every part of my world in order to find my identity again. Unpicking the career path, I had chosen, unpicking the relationship between my partner and I, unpicking the relationship with my family, unpicking the lifestyle I was living, unpicking my health issues, unpicking just about everything in my control. But then, following a series of family bereavements, including the loss of my father, I began not only to question every part of my world, but also to question the world in general. And this was when the magic happened.

Here I was, working the nine to five, conforming with what the world told me I needed to do to be successful. I educated myself so that I could work. I worked to pay my mortgage, to have nice holidays and drive a nice car, to have a pension, to be desirable enough to find a decent partner so we could get married and start a family, so that we could raise children to be educated, to work...and so the cycle continues. And even writing this now makes me feel uncomfortable, because I, like most others, have been conditioned to believe that this is how life 'should' be. We become attached to this notion, and it becomes so intrinsically interwoven into society that it becomes the 'norm', and anything outside of this model ends up being considered an 'alternative' lifestyle. Yet, when you look at all these things, I mean really look at them, they're all materialistic, learned 'norms' that keep humans under control, and they all revolve around money. It is often said that money makes the world go around, and sadly we do live in a society now where this is the case. Our lives literally depend on money now. So where did it all go wrong?

Now, don't get me wrong, I have a mortgage and I'm married with a daughter, I like money and holidays, and I want the nice cars. But, here's the trick: "I want the nice cars." Study that sentence for a minute.

Amongst all the soul searching and the questioning, I realised something. Something very significant that changed my outlook and fundamentally changed the way I look at the world and my life. I realised the difference between *want* and *need*. Somebody said to me recently "I always taught my children to think about whether they really needed something or not, because we can't always get what we want." Does this sound familiar? And yes, this helps children with understanding boundaries and self-control, but as an adult, here's my challenge to this: Why can't we always get what we want? And, what is wrong with getting what we want? Think about those two questions before you read on.

To *need* something is to focus on its absence, the fear of not having it. For example, I need a new car because: I hate my car! It is unreliable; I need to be able to get places; it will make me happy; I will feel complete when I get it; without it I am miserable; when I drive my current car I just hate it; when I see other people with the car I want I am envious; my friends have nice cars and I need one too.

These are the kinds of stories you can tell yourself when you *need* something.

To *want* something is to focus on having it. For example, I want a new car because: I love new cars! It would be great to have a car I can rely on; I would love to be able to get to places more easily; new cars smell nice; it will feel great driving something new and shiny; and I can show it off to my friends. But if I don't get one, it doesn't matter because mine can always be fixed and I will always be able to get places. I can just smell my friend's new car!

Do you see the difference? By *wanting* something the energy shifts from a negative desperation to have something that will fulfil my self-worth, to a positive desire to have something that I remain unattached to, thus my happiness and self-worth remain unaffected.

The reality is that the only things we *need* are oxygen, food, water and warmth. Everything else is a *want*. And once I learned this my whole world started changing because my outlook became so much more positive. I began *wanting* things. I found the more I *wanted* the more I got because I shook all attachment to not having them. And this doesn't stop at the material. I found my truth and happiness in being single. Instead of searching for the partner I *needed* to make me complete, I searched for the partner I *wanted* to complement my completeness. I learned that there's nothing in this world that I *need* that can bring me happiness because I already have happiness. But there are plenty of things that I *want* that can complement that happiness.

Once I threw my learned beliefs about *wanting* and *needing* out of the window, I soon realised that I can challenge any of my beliefs and change how I feel about them. I learned that "Things like this don't happen to me" isn't my truth, and that when *things like this* do happen to me, that they're catalysts for my greater good. I learned that "I am not an emotional person" was something I was taught. For example, as a child being told to stop being a 'squinny' (this is local dialect for 'cry baby'), or when I got older, the typical 'Stiff upper lip' and 'Man up' responses to emotions weren't at all part of my truth, and that being emotional is hugely therapeutic and healing. I learned that "I have failed" was purely my definition and that I simply needed to redefine what *failure* meant, or even if I believed in failure at all. I learned that my job doesn't define me, nor do I need to allow any job to break me ever again. I learned that when "I felt utterly hopeless", it was purely based on my self-worth and definition of failure, so I now choose to believe differently. I choose to believe that there is always hope and that everything is part of my journey to my greatest potential, no matter how bumpy the ride. And when you learn this, when you learn to undo what you've been led to believe and choose to believe what works for you, you can truly live the life of your dreams.

But it doesn't end there. You may be thinking that this is all well and good, but it's all very 'Western' and doesn't make me a decent human being, just a greedier one. And again, this is where I want you to challenge your thoughts. If you had more of what you want, would you be in a better place to help others? If you lived your greatest potential, would your story inspire others? If life was that little bit easier for you, what would you do with your spare time/money/resources? The age-old saying of "Charity begins at home" isn't just an over-used quote, it's a truth that I choose to believe. Do you?

I know I make all this sound simple but, believe me, it's a journey and it takes practice, more than that, it takes patience. So never beat yourself up for stumbling, taking a few back pedals, or even giving up. It's simply part of your path and, when you're ready, you will continue to your greatest potential. Right now, I'm just showing you where the path is, it's up to you how far you go.

I hope you enjoyed my story and, even by just taking one word of inspiration from it, I hope you can find that your greatest potential is already within you.

HAPPY MONDAY NAMASTE

Paul Elliot

Dear Reader,

Be in love, be in love with you. How you feel about yourself affects your mood, your health and your life. Be in love with music, the quickest way to change your mood, your health and your life. Be in love with that person in the mirror, the most important person in your life.

Never feel worthless. Everything you are made of you will find in the universe. This is where you were born. What an amazing feat of engineering, what a magical being you are.

Never let anyone destroy your peace and beauty, for you are a unique being made by the Universe. Problems and worries are only lessons teaching you that you can overcome anything you set your mind to.

It is a feeling you should never let go of because it is yours. Keep it close to you.

When it is a part of you, it belongs to you. This will give form to your life and to the life of others.

This wonderful energy will surround you and you will attract people who feel the same.

It is a pleasant energy, so it will provide you with happiness. You will never be alone. They love to linger in it.

You will be capable of achieving anything.

When you are in love with yourself, you will accept yourself as you are.

You will know that you are special. No need to compare yourself with others because you will be happy with who you are.

This will take time and effort. It will not happen overnight.

Start today with accepting who you are and to love yourself for it.

FROM FRUSTRATION TO FREEDOM

Phillipa Clark

Dear Reader,

It was a Monday morning and was looking forward to going to work. Yes, looking forward to going to work. "Why?" you might ask? After another turbulent weekend of arguments and upset with my husband, it was a welcome relief to be with my work friends and be distracted. After the upset of my first marriage failing and being left with two small children and a broken heart, I thought I'd found my happy-ever-after when I met my second husband. How wrong I was.

Looking back, I should have seen the signs. The trouble is, I'm a fixer. At least, that's what

I used to be in my past relationships. I used to give far more than I received. I saw the best in people, which helped me justify their behaviours.

Well, this Monday was different. I finally made a change that my heart and soul needed. I'd put on my big girl's pants by telling my husband that I wasn't going to put up with his behaviour anymore because I was done with being so unhappy.

It was like an epiphany. Finally, I had said what I'd been pondering on for months. When the words came out, I was shocked. I thought, "You haven't thought this through. You can't take it back now." It didn't matter. I felt empowered yet scared at the same time.

We talked things through, which was strange and weird, but I knew there would be no turning back as I'd been feeling like this for a long while. In fact, until I'd said it, I didn't realise the extent of my unhappiness. I knew with all my heart that I'd finally set myself free.

Timing wise, it wasn't the best. But when is a good time? I'd just gone fully self-employed at the end of July and this was September. How was I going to cope? What will happen? Will my children be upset? What will people think? What will my family say? I'm a failure – I can't even stay married the second time. I'm stupid for thinking I can do this now. A million other negative thoughts raced around my head. I didn't sleep well that night and cried myself to sleep.

Looking back, it was a mixture of relief, shock and disbelief that I'd finally had the courage to do it. So, that Monday was the start of my new life.

I was lucky as I had some amazing friends at work, and they were brilliant. My family, on the other hand, were not. When I told them, the response was, "Surely, you could try to make it work." The irony of this is, when my husband and I had spilt up the previous year for different reasons (husband was sex texting), they told me how much they didn't like him from day one. It didn't seem to matter to them that he was a flirt, a big drinker, suffered from extreme mood swings, anxiety and depression or made me unhappy. The unsaid message was, "How dare you bring shame on us. Our daughter can't even stay married the second time around." I hadn't expected anything more, as they had never been the supportive parents I would've liked. I had told them out of courtesy.

My friends were different. If it wasn't for their love and support, I'm not sure I would have got through it. I'm very grateful I have them in my life.

You may ask, "What changed? Why did you decide to say how you felt and end your marriage?" To be honest, I'm not sure what the final straw was. However, it wasn't an out of the blue feeling. I now know it was my soul calling for me to break free.

When I first met him, he wooed me by being a complete charmer. At the time, my self-esteem was at rock bottom because of my first marriage having ended due to my ex having an affair. I was feeling unlovable and insecure. So, when he gave me so much attention and seemed so different from my first husband, I fell for him hook, line and sinker.

As I said, looking back, I should have seen that he wasn't the most stable and trustworthy of men. However, love is blind. After getting engaged, within the year, I'd agreed to move to be with him. I knew if I moved within a certain timeframe that it would be less upsetting for my children.

Ever since I was a little, I've had an affinity with the sea, it's my happy place. By moving area, I got to live by the sea. We managed to get my dream house (now I know I manifested it, but I didn't at the time). Life was going to be good, a fresh start for all of us.

It was scary in the new area at first, not knowing anyone and juggling work with childcare. In fact, I'd underestimated just what affect change has on you. Now, not surrounded by friends or family, it was me, my two children and my fiancé. This sacrifice was never acknowledged by him. To make it worse, he dealt with the change by going out on big drinking benders and keeping me at a distance. This was August, and in September, I was starting a college course to train to be a counsellor and hypnotherapist.

Really, the move and starting the course were the start of me transforming, the start of the real me emerging. In December that year, I left my job of 14 years in the corporate world as the commute was getting too much and I really didn't enjoy it or fit in any more. I knew I was different, but not sure why. I took on a job in a completely different area, which was local and perfect for me. The following April, we got married and even then, I was beginning to doubt my decision, but didn't tell anyone what I was thinking.

What followed was a rocky, turbulent relationship. It was filled with money problems, having to deal with an alcoholic (who wouldn't admit he was one) flirting with other women, arguments resulting in lots of sleepless nights, tears and upset. Once again, my self-esteem was rock bottom. I felt such failure. Why couldn't I get it right? Why is everyone else so happy and in love?

The universe has a way of making you deal with things, which at the time can make you feel as if you're being ripped open. It's when we're at rock bottom that we can find our own inner strength. That inner light that may have been dimmed for so long. That flicking of your soul that wants to shine brightly like it's meant to.

A conversation I had one day sparked my interest in the law of attraction and other spiritual things. I'd always been different growing up as I was interested in astrology, aromatherapy and crystals. I knew my beliefs were not conventional but now there was so much more information around thanks to the internet. I soaked it up like a sponge. What immense relief it was knowing that there was a bigger picture and that all the pain and suffering I'd experienced in my life happened for me not to me.

After the initial spark, which helped me start to transform, I found knowing and understanding about angels, archangels and our own guardian angels changed my life. I love knowing angels are there to help, even with little things like getting a parking space and that the universe is loving and encourages me to be who I chose to be in this lifetime. Finally, everything made sense.

Through training in hypnotherapy and understanding how the mind works, including how it can hold you back without you really understanding why, I've been able to deal with a lot of my underlying beliefs and issues. I feel that my journey to find me began without me even knowing what was happening. I woke up to life and the beauty within me. It was this awakening and my soul calling out that helped me to muster the courage to leave my second marriage.

I'm not going to lie and say it has all been smooth sailing since that eventful day. However, I'm not the same person as I was back then. I'm happy with myself. I have the power within to overcome whatever challenges come my way because I'm strong, and I'm loved more than I will ever know.

It's by being in the dark that I have learnt to look for the light and I'm fortunate to be in a position in which I can help others take steps to begin their journeys. I realise that we're all connected, we're all one and that the most important thing in the whole universe is Love.

Despite all the heartache, I still believe one-hundred per cent in true love and I know divine timing will lead me to my 'one' when the time is right. In the meantime, I'm happy being me. I trust and believe in the universe and that nothing happens by chance. I'm blessed and love all the people in my life who light up my soul. If I hadn't started making the changes to really understand myself, seeing the patterns I created and how untrue my inner programming was, I would still be stuck in a very unhappy marriage and doing a job I hated.

If you're in a dark place, feeling like there's no way out, believe me there is. You just must ask yourself and listen. The universe, God, angels or whatever you believe in will help you if you ask them. Be open that the help will arrive in all manner of ways. You might see a post on Facebook, buy a magazine and read an article or someone might say something to you in a flippant comment. Even reoccurring numbers have meaning. Always know that they'll answer you and be open to whatever arrives.

I did a vision board the year I finally split up with my husband and one of the things I'd put on my board was that I wanted a 'happy & loving relationship'. Obviously, that was never going to happen with him. The universe answered me by helping me gain the courage to leave my unhappy relationship in order to open the way for a new happy relationship to arrive. It wasn't until afterwards that I could see that.

I now talk all the time to my angels and guides, meditate to gain guidance, practice gratitude, use the moon to put out my intentions to the universe and release what's no longer serving me. I love using my crystals, reading and learning more. My psychic abilities have grown immensely. My trust in the universe and divine timing has been tested, but always the universe delivers in miraculous ways.

I fully believe that I'm on the right path now as I love my role as 'A Shining Light' to help others. Plus, I'm lucky to have some gorgeous like-minded souls around me that I call family. They're not physically related but they're how family should be. I'm now the director of my own play and I'm going to dream big and aim for the stars.

Love Philippa x

WORKING FOR MYSELF

Kate Buxton

Dear Reader,

It's Monday morning and it's 9am. I've just woken up, we're in the winter season so I have decreed Monday as a day of rest. It's my Monday and I'm going to enjoy it. After a few episodes of American sitcoms on the television and the tea my husband makes for me every morning, I decide it's time to scrape myself through the shower.

I also have decreed that Tuesdays be a day off as well, so my weekend has started.

It's quite nice to have two days off in the week when everyone else is working. Though you do tend to meet other people, those who have the joy of being their own bosses, who make similar decrees. Hump day, Wednesday, is the new Monday and before you know it the week has gone, which is great!

Another marvellous thing about working for myself is that I have the joy of plotting and scheming what I'm going to do for the year. It's always top secret, rarely straightforward, and occasionally requiring the help of others. I've realised that you soon find the connections you require to get all your tasks done and meet some lovely people along the way.

For those who have said to you "you can't" or "it will never work", I have advice for you:

1. It blummin' well will if you want it to and you will become an expert manifestor in no time at all. Visualise what you want and if it's for your highest good, it will happen. If it gets too difficult, or if there are too many closed doors, start running and go to plan B.

2. Always have a plan B and a plan C.

3. You don't have to go it alone or aim to have it all at once. Start small and aim for the sky. Before you know it, you will have an empire!

4. It doesn't matter what others think of you. The only person who makes it a problem is you, so snap out of it!

5. Do what makes you happy, not what everyone else thinks you 'should' be doing. Oh, and get that word 'should' out of your vocabulary. Replace it with phrases like... "It would be preferable if"

and "perhaps it would work better this way". Just watch how the energy of your speech changes, and how different the reactions from people are. It's a much more positive frame.

Procrastination is my demon, I will run one-hundred per cent away from anything that needs doing in a sensible, timely fashion. All the while, my Virgo ascendant is saying: 'by the gods woman, get it done and put it in a nice little box with a bow, miles ahead of time. Spit-spot and Bristol fashion'. I've never found a cure, but I have quite often found its timing on a situation just isn't right, or something else isn't right and doesn't fit: the cogs aren't falling in together and the gears are being ground to Hades and back.

So here we go on to my old friend patience. My Aries moon wants it all to happen yesterday, and it's a lesson I get over and over. Working for yourself, it's all about Divine timing: opportunities popup when you least expect them and it's a case of grabbing them by the horns even if they scare the pants off you!

Look for signs to guide you along the way. I work shamanicaly. So, for me, I'm always looking for signs. This has just happened as I write. I have just had a flock of seagulls (the seagull is one of my power animals) serenade me, with one bird sitting on the roof opposite, staring bolt at me just to make sure I get the message that I'm on the right track. Signs could be feathers or coins on the floor, the sun coming out at an opportune moment or a big gust of wind. I have a habit of going cold when something is bang on right. My spiritual practice helps guide my business.

Some people work with the moon to help bring abundance and get rid of things that hold them back. There's no harm in writing down what your plans are for the year then burning them or burying them on a new moon. It's surprising the results it brings. Always use the intent of things being for your highest good. if things don't work out the way you expect then you can take great comfort in knowing that it just wasn't meant to be and if you had forced the issue vast problems would have come from it.

Another thing I have found is not to be too greedy. It's great if we can build an empire and have loads of money, but it won't bring you happiness. I ask for enough money to pay my bills and have a little bit extra. As an example, my shop money is for stock, rent and all the boring stuff. When there is some left over for me that's fab. I do readings and healing too, this is my bunce money, so there's my enough to cover bills and a little bit extra.

Stay humble, folks. However big you think your first-world problems are, there's always someone else with bigger ones or the situation could be so much worse than it is. Plus, there's always a way out of it. I would use Ho'oponopono on anything that seems impossible. It's so powerful and works in unexpected ways.

Get a good accountant. Apart from being

great at 'creative' accounting, accountants take away the stress of numbers. I'm practically number blind, which could stop me from moving forward. Thankfully, I was blessed with logic and a good pair of hands with some creativity thrown in. Don't let anything hold you back, there's a way around everything. Thank the gods for spellcheck or else you would be reading reverse words all over the place.

It doesn't matter what skill set you have, you will have a huge one by going it alone. You don't have to be psychic to work out what you want to do and then how to get it. If you want to work for yourself, yes, it's hard work and businesses can take a while to build up, but, by the gods, it's worth it.

Knowing when to take a break is vital. Before you know it, you have been to work, which in my case is my shop, then come home and sat on the computer all night doing promotion or websites etc. Stop right there! Manage your time, keep calm and walk away from the laptop. Or before you know it, you will be working all the hours that the gods send and have a small work addiction problem. I can think of better things to be addicted to. Get some exercise, go for a walk to the park and feed the birds.

Know when to give in. Yes, give in. That's a tough one which must be learned. You are not the bionic woman or man, if your body is saying 'I just can't' or on the flips side, 'the timing isn't perfect, but the situation is', compromise. Listen to your gut.

I will spend a few words on the green-eyed monster, jealousy. When you have something good or it's going to be good, other people will want it, try to get in on it, or try to bring you down because they feel threatened. That's their insecurity, not yours. You're a strong individual and you've got this. I've found working alone to be most beneficial when it comes to this. Yes, it's batshit scary at times but I answer to no one which is worth its weight in gold.

And take the time to thank the universe when things are going well, how else will it know it's got it right?

It's all worth it though when your business-baby is up and running and the start of your empire has begun!

If I can do this then you most definitely can.

Best of luck reader, may the gods be with you.

BEAUTY IN THE BREAKDOWN

Renee Furlow

Dear Reader,

It's Monday morning and I have an overwhelming amount of emotions today.

She sits and wonders how she got to this point. Away from all that is familiar, stripped of all that is known and once thought to be needed, she lays down and closes her eyes. Those voices that steered her too far off course. The surrounding people that didn't understand. Wanting to be heard but scared to yell. She had been bent so far that she broke. She broke down and was now segregated in a world surrounded by the unknown – no other words to describe what was going on except that she was in the process of a complete breakdown.

Pushed to the limits, she realizes that it's okay to feel this way. It's okay to feel lost at times. It's okay to ask for help. It's okay to say no, it doesn't make a person less than a person. Basically, people are just not okay all the time, and even that's okay. Praying and lost in thought, she seeks and finds complete solace within herself. Stripped of all that she felt she had to have to survive, she finds herself in the darkness and somehow finds clarity and sense.

Does the above sound like a total breakdown? I don't think so. I think we're all in different places on our journeys. We all fight battles in different ways. Some of us need a time-out, others react in different ways – no one is alone in this. This awareness will come to us at the right time and place. It's important to treat each other with respect and to just understand. Each person has a different perspective on life in their gorgeous uniqueness.

> *"I may have not gone where I intended to go, but I think I wound up where I needed to be." – Douglas Adams*

No one expects to wind up in the middle of a breakdown. However, life can throw you curve balls and put you on a different course. That was me. I had a life planned out that I thought was going to work. I did everything I could, made some mistakes along the way, but overall felt great about the way I was living. Then, I let someone in my head. I let this person tamper with my sense of reality. Instead of listening to what I knew to be true – my intuition and my gut instinct – I chose to listen outside of me, and it sent me over. Coming from a broken environment, it was my every intention to never live that way again. Somehow, it still caught up with me and I, as stated above, broke.

"Crazy is not about being broken or swallowing a dark secret. It's you or me – amplified ... Was I ever crazy? Maybe I was - or maybe I was just a girl, interrupted." -
Susanna Kayson

The definition of the word 'crazy' is as follows: mad, insane, deranged, and demented. Now, would you honestly use any of those words to describe someone you know or even yourself? I don't think so. Labelling one as 'crazy' does nothing good for them. It can hurt and make one feel isolated from the rest of the world because they are so 'different'.

"Some people are beautiful. Not in looks. Not what they say. Just in what they are." -
Markus Zusak

On a road of recovery, I've been blessed beyond words by the gorgeous people I've met. The kindred spirits I've met have been very inspiring and have helped me forward in some way. Even if it seemed like what was going on at the time was not the best thing to go through, it still led to pure beauty. Life, as I am living it, is so very exhilarating. Part of the beauty I see in others, and what I see in me, is due to the happiness on their faces, the love in their hearts and the feelings in their heads.

> *"Leave your things behind,*
> *because it's all going off*
> *without you." – Imogen Heap*

Want to know a pretty awesome secret for utter bliss? Don't carry your baggage with you every place you go. Just like you place a book down after it has been read, and it's likely not to be picked up again, why would you keep dragging things around? At any point, the details of your life can be changed. There's a reason you're here and there's a gorgeousness about you because you've made it through a dark time and come out ahead.

Don't let things happen to you. Change your mindset to think that life is happening for you. The elegance of your uniqueness is an elegance this world needs.

> *"You can't take anything for*
> *granted for a second otherwise*
> *you trip up. More than*
> *anything, I believe life is all*
> *about timing. I know certainly*
> *every situation in my life has*
> *been like "why now?" and it's*
> *a test or a beautiful moment.*

That's why life is so gorgeous."
-- Lena Headey

Something is to be said about the ones that have overcome adversity and hardship. We all have a journey in this world and each one of us has our own signature style. The absolute artistry life creates with each one of us is exquisite. Things would not be the same without you in this world. We all are connected. We all make a difference. We all matter. We're all worthy. And we're all enough. That is such a beautiful realization to come to.

There is pure beauty in life, and it plans for us all. We're all connected and doing the best we can, with what we have and what we know in the here and now. Your struggles, your triumphs, sad, mad and glad moments – they're all unique. And the more we respect each other, the better we all will be - no one does it alone.

"Someone gave me a box of
darkness. It took me years to.
understand that this, too, was
a gift." - Mary Oliver

So, the past breakdown may have been hard to go through, and it might have not seemed like there would be light again. But there is light once more. It's shining bright, glowing and radiating. And this time, it's not coming from the outside, it's from the inside. All these reasons and so many more are why I trust in, believe in and know deep in my heart ...... There is true beauty in the breakdown.

THE DISILLUSIONED LIGHTWORKER

Genevieve Robson

Dear Reader,

It's Monday morning and we're starting the week afresh; with a whole new set of choices and a whole new set of opportunities. We're all being called to help our fellow men and women. One of the ways that we can do this is by being a lightworker

People often think a lightworker has a profound calling such as being a healer, psychic or medium. In fact, it has very little to do with what you do for a job and far more to do with how you lead your life. Being a lightworker can be as simple as sharing positivity, being kind, being compassionate, leading your life as an example to others or serving humanity and planet earth.

We may also choose to express our light by teaching, writing, healing, counselling or enlightening others. As you can see, these things aren't mutually exclusive to lightworkers.

Being a lightworker isn't always an easy path but it can be tremendously rewarding. Over the years, I've come across many lightworkers and holistic practitioners that have walked away because they have either become disillusioned or they are lacking in self-belief to such an extent that they turn away from their calling of helping people.

It's here that I'll discuss this topic by shedding light on the reasons why people become disillusioned with their paths and how to overcome it. At any given moment, each of us makes decisions about how we choose to live our lives. In doing so, we co-create our world with the universe. No path is more valid than any other but if you feel drawn to be a lightworker, I hope to help you to understand this path better and stay on it.

My name is Genevieve Robson, I'm a medium and healer. It's my passion to support people to realise their unique abilities and encourage them to develop them. I believe that we all have innate healing and psychic abilities that we can develop to a greater or lesser extent. For some people, this comes naturally but for others, these abilities need to be developed by applying themselves to this pursuit. I don't believe that only 'special people' can do these things as I've witnessed people with little or no experience demonstrating profound healing and psychic abilities. I always advocate that my students find their own proof and come to their own conclusions by following their own unique paths. I encourage students to perceive things for themselves. This, in turn, gives them the evidence they need to make their own minds up.

My story isn't a unique one. I grew up in an environment in which it was the norm to be psychic. As a teenager, my mother told me about the experiences of seeing ghosts and deja vu. I started teaching friends to meditate when I was 14-years-old. I had many interesting experiences including precognitive dreams, astral travel, psychic insights and communication with spirit. However, I was lacking somebody that could explain what I was experiencing. I didn't learn the terms 'medium', 'psychic' or 'healer' until years later, so I couldn't research what was happening to me.

During this time, I became frightened about these things and I closed off from it all. In my early twenties, I had a spiritual dream that prompted me to go to a spiritualist church and ask to develop my abilities. Looking back on it now, I realise what a shame it was that I closed off from this inherent part of myself.

My development was arduous due to my own personal blocks. It was also tremendously rewarding, uplifting, supportive and awe-inspiring. I learnt from many teachers and read everything I could get my hands on. My blocks included being rational, analytical, fearful of the unknown and struggling with self-doubt. I spent time working on my own blocks.

Now, I support my students to perceive more by first working on their own blocks. In my own development, I got to the point where I was able to deliver evidence to strangers but couldn't perceive things for myself. It's a common trait amongst healers and mediums to have blockages in giving themselves these things. Therefore, I strongly recommend that healers heal themselves and that mediums receive messages for themselves. For me, learning to listen to my intuition has been revolutionary and it has helped me with all aspects of my life. These blocks that lightworkers experience often are contributing reasons for them walking away. The tools they need to overcome these blocks aren't hard to master, especially if they consider the benefits.

Some lightworkers become disappointed when they don't attain instant results but find what they're seeking doesn't develop or is slow to develop. This is purely because they haven't practiced enough or learned how to work with this energy. Thoughts are energy. If they have beliefs such as "I can't do this, only special people can be psychic or a healer etc" and "Other people are better at this than I am" this causes an energetic block. Everything in life that's worthwhile needs effort and commitment. The same is true here.

I love the Eureka moment when the light bulb goes off in their heads and they perceive something amazing or overcome their blocks. It's my passion to help people learning to channel these energies develop an understanding of what their unique abilities are and how to use them. I help people to develop their abilities by explaining the principles behind energy work. I explain the different methods they can use to experience them for themselves.

Mediumship and healing both work on the principal that you are channelling energy from Source, the Universe or God on behalf of your client. As a medium, you're channelling information to convey to your client and as a healer you're channelling energy to the client to promote their own healing.

I believe that no matter where you are in your spiritual journey that you only ever glimpse a small percentage of your full potential. It's your choice if you want to develop these abilities further. Wherever you are in your journey, there's information and experiences that will enhance your connection to all life and your ability to perceive the hidden but undeniable truth. I'm not speaking of something make-believe or unreal. I mean opening to quantifiable and tangible information accessible to all that pursue it. This energy is all around us and is only 'hidden' because we haven't learnt to perceive it yet. I believe that we're all able to perceive these things for ourselves and understand the fundamental principles involved.

You can learn to use your psychic senses to perceive more of life than you currently do by developing your clairvoyance (seeing), clairaudience (hearing), clairsentience (feeling), and claircognizance (knowing). The word clair means clear and voyance means vision. We learn to tap into a heightened state of awareness. In doing so, we can look beyond the physical world and tap into the energy that underpins all of life. We're able to perceive information about the past, present and future relating to objects, places, people or animals.

Many people become disillusioned because they are unable to perceive more, but like any other skill it can be developed by practicing. Others become disillusioned because they can't see or hear. This doesn't concern me as I always encourage my students to use whatever sense they are currently working with and let their other senses develop with time. Rather than focusing on what my students can't do yet, I always encourage them to work on their strengths as their weaker areas will develop with time.

I'm mindful of the words we use, so rather than students saying, "I cannot see" or "I'm not clairvoyant", I always encourage them to add "yet". That way they don't block themselves from sensing or seeing more in the future. The best way to judge if you're indeed able to perceive things outside of the normal realms of possibility is to sit in a psychic development circle and see if you can sense facts about a total stranger. Development circles are common in Britain, with most spiritualist churches hosting one. Spiritual churches are one of many routes that you can go down. No single path is better than the other. I do encourage students to learn from lots of different teachers and to make their own minds up about what suits them best.

Energy healing takes one of two forms. One is the channelling of energy from the Universe/God or Source to the patient and the other is that of removing energy from the patient when it no longer serves them or is causing a blockage.

Some healing practitioners struggle getting results as the person needs stuck energy to be removed before the new energy can do its work. It's important to say that any energy being removed needs to be replaced, the space needs to be filled in with Universal, God or Source energy.

It doesn't matter if you're doing Reiki, Rahanni, Spiritual healing, Shamanic healing, etc, as they all come from the same Source. They have fundamentally different concepts, applications and deliveries but ultimately, they're all aided by the same principles. The healing energy can be applied to people, animals, buildings, landscapes and situations.

Healers need to be aware of the placebo effect. The placebo effect is psychogenic, but it can induce measurable changes in the body. The placebo effect is important to understand when dealing with physical illnesses that are believed to arise from emotional or mental stressors. These are called psychogenic disease or psychogenic illness. It's important to recognise that not only emotions and energy have an impact on a person's health and healing, but we can also use our words and body language to help heal a person. We can do this by speaking and acting with confidence. We can help the person although we cannot guarantee the healing will help energetically emotionally or physically. We cannot guarantee the results, we can only channel the energy.

Likewise, we need to be aware of the nocebo effect which is detrimental to physical health and caused by psychological factors such as negative expectations of treatment or prognosis. In order to avoid hurting our patients, we need to be positive in front of them, regardless of how dire their prognosis or situation is. We need to be positive about their medical treatment and never suggest they stop taking any medication or treatment prescribed by their doctor. By understanding the placebo and nocebo effects, we can help more people. In turn, it can stop healers from walking away because they don't understand how energy works.

Many people become disillusioned because they see other 'spiritual people' acting in non-spiritual ways. There may be lots of politics at their spiritual centres or they may not be following their own codes of practice. I try to keep out of other people's dramas, understanding it's their journey and I can only be responsible for my own actions. These things, after all, are part of the human condition.

When I teach people to develop, I don't try to make them a carbon copy of me. Instead, I show them lots of different methods that I've learnt over the years so they can choose which one works the best for them. I encourage them to follow their own path. There are many students that have moved from other groups because they were affected by the politics. Some of the politics eventually erode spiritual groups. People leave and just give up, thinking that all spiritual groups are like this.

Students have swapped to my circle because their previous circle didn't have enough practice. My circles are disciplined but they're supportive. The circle begins with a meditation and then the students spend the rest of the time practicing the techniques for themselves.

I always say to my groups that they need to understand energy and how things work spiritually. In addition, they need to understand and work on themselves in order to progress. Healers and mediums often look after others to the detriment of themselves. The more you work on and heal yourself the more you will be able to help others, be a positive example and channel higher vibrational energies.

I don't feel that being a lightworker is for everyone. Nor do I feel that my views or opinions are more valid than anyone else's. Instead, I ask you to look at what you want from life and consciously inform yourself of options.

Whatever decisions you make now, know that you can choose at any given moment how you want your life to be. Understanding energy and working your light will help you to do this. I only want to convey how much solace, upliftment, guidance and joy being a healer and medium has brought me over the years.

As you progress with the week ahead think of me working to support my community in Portsmouth, England. Take a moment to reflect on all the ways that you encourage and support those around you.

A SACRED MORNING

Susan Thames

Dear Reader,

It's Monday morning and the donkey just brayed out the breakfast call, but the Collies are snoring on the rug beside the bed. I pull the quilt over my head. Please, I would so love to go back to sleep under the warm covers. Nope, not to happen. One cold nose slips under the blanket, "You know it is time to get up and start another wonderful day." That's Belle, the youngest. Chi, the ancient (pushing 15 in doggie years is 'old' in human reckoning), paws at the bed. *Up now*, time to get *up now*.

Okay, okay! I love to be awakened to doggie kisses and wagging tails. We stumble toward the kitchen. Girls, out the living-room door to potty, heat water for tea for me, fill dog bowls with crumbles for my furry loves. Back in the kitchen door for breakfast. Sniff, sniff, sniff at the bowls full of crumbles. Both shaggy black and white ladies of luxury head to their doggie beds, breakfast untouched. I suppose, when you're privileged, pampered and totally spoiled just knowing breakfast has been served is sufficiently acceptable. After all, maybe Monday at 6am is even too early in doggiedom.

With a sigh of resignation, I find my comfy living room chair, sip my lovely cup of hot tea and read from my bardic grade Gwers (That's a lesson in druid speak). I'm just about to finish my bardic year of training with the Order of Bards, Ovates, and Druids. I've found my home. Oh, apologies. I love my physical home, a small farm in Northeast Texas. I meant my spiritual home. They send me lessons that lead me out on the land in reverence and ceremony. Always blessing, in all ways grateful. Following the Wheel of the Year as ancient pre-historic ancestors did many moons ago. Gazing up at the same Mother Moon and seeing what those druid priests and priestesses saw in the velvety blue-black night sky. Following her progress through time, watching the stars twinkle and the wisps for clouds dance across her face. Ah, there I go, my thoughts wandering poetically, such a bard thing to do.

Okay, tea sipped, lesson read, and now there's enough light to walk to the barn without tripping over a skunk or other small creature. Please stop. Smell the freshness of the air. Cool, crisp with hints of frost, hay and horses lingering on the breeze. Oak leaves wet and shining with tiny crystalline castles of frost. Father Sun is making his morning appearance casting pastel light all around. Lingering on the southern horizon, grey clouds touched with pink. Once again, the donkey brays the breakfast alarm. "Okay, I'm coming," I mumble to three horses and a donkey, heads up, alert, anticipating their breakfast of a horsey granola mixture and sweet coastal hay. Have you ever watched horses eat? They love their food. They munch away happily with looks of ecstasy on their long equine faces. Soft whiskered lips savouring every crumble. How much healthier would we be if we enjoyed our breakfasts as much?

Cats burst through the barn door at a run, to start a day of chasing small moving creatures and basking in the sun. That's what cats do best. Soak up sun shine until their fur smells sweet and warm. The chickens are fed. Such appreciation for a small handful or two of grain. Strutting and clucking happily over titbits found here and there.

"Okay, girls are you ready for a walk? Let's go for a walk," I say. Wagging tails, running in front of me, finding our well-worn path. First, we visit the pond. Take a moment to look at the reflection of the morning sky on the mirror surface of the water. Breath taking beauty reflected to us. Baby blue, pink, touches of yellow. A minnow breaks the surface, causing concentric rings that go on and on. Sometimes, the Blue Heron is standing on the edge of the pond and will honk out a reproachful greeting. According to the *Animal Medicine Cards* created by Jamie Sams and David Carson, Blue Heron is about self-reflection. "Heron medicine is the power of knowing the self by discovering it's gifts and facing its challenges."

I choose to acknowledge the small things in life as my gifts, such as the dogs, a good cup of tea, an adventure with Cousin Sandra and this piece of land we live on and love dearly. Challenges come and go. In the moment, they can overwhelm us and cause us worry and frustration. Challenges can literally scare us to death. We can feel like we are riding a wild tornado, touching down here and there, causing destruction with no control. Then the winds will die down and the challenge is over. What to do with the aftermath? Wallow in self-pity or hitch up our britches, dust off the seats of our pants, kick the mud off our boots and like the Fool of the tarot, set out once again into the unknown. Joyous to get on with the adventure!

From the pond we walk to the fence, take a right, then another right along a tree line creek. When Chi was younger, we would splash our way across the creek. Old age with creaky joints, deafness and an unstable gait makes the steep descent to the creek dangerous for her. So, we alter our course for a bit, and that's okay. That's what you do for those you love. Someday, Belle and I will once

151

again splash through the creek. That will be a sad day. My heart hurts just thinking of the day we will no longer have our beautiful Chi leading us on forest adventures, splashing across creeks, chasing smart aleck squirrels and once again finding the path back home and into our hearts.

But Chi is with us today. And it's a beautiful morning. Turn your face to the sky, smile. Hear crow and blue jay call a warning. Look, the cats have accompanied us on our adventure. Okay, now take a left around these cedars and head straight back towards the fence. See the circle that's created by those old oaks and fallen limbs. That's my sacred grove. My place to worship the creator, the god and goddess, the universal powers that be. Let there be peace throughout the whole world, a few quick words of thank you and a moment taken to watch the sunrise over the hayfield that runs along our eastern fence. My morning bardic practice is done.

Okay, girls, we need to head home. We walk a bit slower on the way to the house. Stopping to look for chickweed and yarrow, two old friends that start making their appearance this time of year. Our morning ritual is about done, our precious time together before the work a day world calls us to tend to the needs of those who, well, need us. The Collies are tired but happy, now it's time for breakfast. They take long slurping drinks from the big water bowl while I make another cup of tea. Breakfast, a shower, gather phone, iPad, lunch, mail, and anything else needed for the day. As I pull out of our long country driveway, I always say a word or two of thanks. I'm so blessed. Yes, it is Monday, my work week starts again.... but I get to come home to unconditional love and the knowledge that tomorrow, I once more will be awakened by a wet nose and wagging tails and the natural world will await to greet me as we step out of the door for our sunrise ramble around the pasture and into the woods.

MONDAYS: FROM MEDIEVAL TO MAGICAL

Michelle Rene

Dear Reader,

It's Monday morning and I've been contemplating, ironically... Monday. The first day of the workweek. A day full of sturm und drang. A day I liken to the Medieval era. This day is the glorious and glowy Moon's namesake. But is it really? For 47 years, it has been more new moon than full, a Dark Ages of sort, full of overlords, oppression, and dragging myself to a life controlled by others. However, times change. Or rather, I'm changing, and learning to appreciate what Monday has to offer.

Monday and I began our journey together

when I entered kindergarten. Being prodded like a peasant going to work in the fields, it was the first day after the weekend where I had to leave the comfort of my bed and imagination, get up early for school, and be around people. It was a harsh entry into the world.

Years passed and we transitioned from school to work. This might have been a better era for our relationship since I loved making my own money. However, a string of micromanaging, passive-aggressive, and/or narcissistic bosses and insipid tasks led to me hating the day. It became a constant reminder that I had little control over my work life, feeling more peon than team player. Not only did I have to get up early, I dreaded going to the office and often felt physically ill. There were far too many days between Medieval-Monday and Five-O'clock-Friday.

Two and a half years ago brought a new fiefdom. I took a job promising professional growth and work that I enjoyed. The catch: I had to work Tuesday through Saturday for about six months in order to supervise staff and 'whip them into shape.' For as much as I hate Monday, I hate working weekends even more, but the opportunity cost seemed worth the adjustment. Then I began to realize my staff were not slacking and did not need the level of oversight that was stated. The duties pledged to me were given to my new supervisor, and I spent most of my time toiling on reports about what I did over the week and backing up my staff on the phone and counter. Projects I started were taken from me and I wasn't given new ones. Once again, I was locked into a feudal system, as well as lied to about my position and organizational needs. My professional life fell backwards 30 years, and I wondered how to break the dysfunctional cycle of 'vapid-job, insufferable-boss.'

Although my workweek now began on Tuesday, and Monday became my Sunday, this did not improve my attitude. A business day as part of my weekend, on one hand, gave me a day to run errands that did not require using paid time off. Medical appointments, oil changes, trips to the bank, grocery shopping—all were stacked into Monday. During the winter, trips to the laundromat were added to the busy-ness. For everything it was, it was not a day of rest.

This version of Monday also led to my social life evaporating. It was difficult to spend time with loved ones who had Saturdays and Sundays off, and I did not have enough energy for them and me. As an introvert, I needed a day to lie on the field instead of work it and avoided engagements as if they were tinged with the plague.

Monday took on an edge, honed by disappointment, frustration, fatigue, and the constant reminder that I was working in a situation fashioned out of haircloth—it itched and scratched. During this period, my health and creativity dissipated; life as whole became loathsome. To accommodate my supervisor's side-eye if I took time off during work, I made a point to schedule appointments on a Monday, regardless of how I felt. Eventually, the exhaustion I had been experiencing became too heavy to carry and I was unable to function. Desperate, I left early on a Thursday to see a physician's assistant. She gave me a note excusing me from my job for two days and a lab order. My results showed anaemia, which improved with a blood transfusion. I told myself this was a sign and that I would change my professional life.

Weeks later, I saw my general practitioner, who, concerned about my heavy menses, referred me to a gynaecologist. Again, I made sure I had Monday appointments. The gynaecologist suggested a uterine ablation to resolve the menstrual issues and anaemia. I spent months trying to schedule this procedure—for a Monday.

Eventually, it became clear that there were no Mondays and my periods were not improving, so I took a Tuesday appointment. The ablation became a D&C (dilation and curettage) when a mass was found. Two days later, when I was diagnosed with endometrial cancer, I finally realized I was pouring blood, sweat and tears into a field that was not mine.

Monday's edge dulled as I stopped trying to squeeze my health into it, becoming Neither-Here-Nor-There-Day. Doctors were now seen on First-Available-Day and calls were made as needed. I stopped placating my 'oppressors,' prepared for medical leave and lived as if my life depended on it.

When I returned to work after surgery, my

'overlords' changed, and I acquired projects that matched my interests and ambitions. When I discovered I would need radiation Monday through Friday, I was able to adjust my work schedule to align with treatments. Despite fatigue, I found I could accomplish more on a Monday than the other four days combined. I held my ground to keep this current schedule after treatment was over, and my new supervisor agreed.

My organization is closed to the public on Monday. The phones do not ring, no one is at the counter, and the building is mostly devoid of staff. I dive into new skills, projects and tasks without interruption. I focus and breathe. I create. The Dark Ages Day is now an additional day without the energy-depleting, extroverted mask I am forced to wear Tuesday through Friday. Instead of having and needing at least one day to withdraw from the world, I write, cook and spend time with loved ones. Gone is the anxiety and angst. Monday, despite disease, fear and exhaustion, contains magic and light, and now improves my work-life balance.

Waking up early is still a challenge, as is dealing with staff and the public. Monday, though, offers a respite, a kind of reverse-Friday, with its quieter, slower place. I enjoy starting my workweek with productivity and preparing for the following four days, and love having more flexibility on the weekends. Creativity, health, cooking, loved ones, kayaking, and enjoying life in general take precedence over toiling in bureaucratic fields.

I actively engage in my experiences and decide what I will and will not allow. I am owning my power. And part of that power is deriving at least some pleasure from every day, including Mondays.

YOU MATTER

Reba White

Dear Reader,

It's Monday morning and I'm going through a particularly rough patch in my life lately. I dread forcing myself out of bed on a Monday. How I'd love to just stay home and sleep. I seriously don't want to face the day, be an adult, and deal with people... not right now. I wish I could take a long (paid) vacation and forget about life for a while!

BUT... I also have this stubborn streak, a trait that is rather annoying sometimes (to myself as well as to others). However, my stubbornness has saved my butt often. During my dark moments when it really matters the most, my stubborn tenacity will not let me throw in the towel. What I'm trying to say is...

I've become a pro at this depression stuff, and *I will not be beat!* I will not let depression win.

I've struggled with depression and anxiety since childhood. These dark moments are nothing new to me. In my younger years, I was in a pretty disturbing place, often entertaining dark thoughts... thoughts of how worthless I was, how I hated life, how my family would be better off without me, how I didn't want to be here, how I didn't belong, and that hell was life and death was heaven (how messed up is that?) etc. I even turned to self-harm, but I'm older now and over the years, I've learned quite a bit about myself and my dark spells that might help you too:

- Recognise when you're in a depression and admit it when it happens. Admit it, own it... that's the first step to realizing you've got a problem.

- Talk about it. Don't keep it all buried inside to fester and grow, it'll just get worse.

- Get active and get out of the house. Finding things to do, whether it's exercising, window shopping, or seeing a movie, helps get the mind off the negative.

- Do something you enjoy. Immersing myself in my artwork and writing also helps get my mind off negativity. You don't have to be an artist, and it doesn't have to be art... reading also helps. Some people prefer to do yard work, garden, cook, clean house, dance...

whatever it is that you enjoy doing, do it.

- Remember to breathe. Counting my breaths and keeping them slow and deep, calms the mind and helps with anxiety and depression. Just breathe.

- Positive affirmations remind me to keep a positive mindset when I am stressed or depressed.

- Find positive quotes. Sharing positive posts on my Facebook page, Positive Warfare, helps me to think positive, and it feels good to know I can help other people who might be having a difficult time.

- Find the beauty in your day. Look around you and find something that you're grateful for. Is the sky a beautiful shade of blue? Are there flowers blooming near you? Are there children laughing and playing nearby? Can you hear birdsong? Did you just witness a good deed? Is your arthritis a bit better today? Is your breathing a little easier today? Did your dog or cat greet you today?

- Do a good deed; helping others feels good. Hold the door for someone. Pay for someone's coffee. Compliment somebody. Leave an anonymous uplifting note in a public space for someone to find. Volunteer your time and give back to the community.

- Smile, even if you don't want to... find a reason to smile

- Go to work. You have bills to pay and responsibilities. Missing work can cause you even more strife and you don't want that. You need to stay afloat and take care of business.

- Remember you have purpose. Reminding myself that I was created for a purpose helps get me through rough moments. You were created for a purpose, too!

Life can be a bear at times, but I will not allow myself to just give-up, even though part of me would love to. These difficult patches, whether a few small annoying hurdles or deep valleys and tall rocky mountains, are put in our path for a reason. Why? Because we're here in this lifetime for a specific purpose. The difficult periods strengthen us and give us knowledge to be used somewhere, sometime in a future point of our journey to help someone else.

You might ask yourself how that is even possible. You might be telling yourself right now, "I'm nobody. What difference can I make in this world?" Well, how we face our problems, how we react, how we problem solve, and how we bumble our way through our life... set an example. Our existence really does matter. We send ripples out into the universe, whether you realize that or not. We are guides and our experiences serve others. I bet you never thought that your burdens are meant to touch someone else's life in a positive way and assist them on their path.

Our experiences not only touch our family's and friends' lives, but strangers as well. We are meant to verbally share our journey with others when they are struggling themselves, or when they have questions, or when people ask for your assistance with a decision or a task. If you think about it, we provide a service to our family, friends, co-workers, and community. We are here to set an example and to serve, often unbeknownst to us, in very profound ways.

By just existing and living your daily life, going about your own business... you're making a difference to someone, somehow. When other people see you hurting; or when you do a kind deed, or whether you succeed (or fail) at a goal, other people take notice. They may or may not be actively observant, but their subconscious takes note, and their minds file the knowledge away for future reference. You may not realize it, but you are an inspiration to someone, somewhere, right now... and to a future somebody.

The next time you're struggling with depression, anxiety, physical limitations, or just having a bad day, remember... *Ripples...* you are ripples in the universe. Visualize that for just a minute and know that *You do matter*. This world needs you in it. You are essential. So, get up out of that bed, and face the day... you never know how you may touch someone's life today.

Wishing you much love and happiness, Rebecca White (aka Reba)

MY LOVE LETTER TO YOU

Diana Sass

"You were put on this earth to achieve your greatest self, to live out your purpose, and to do it courageously."

— *Steve Maraboli, Life, the Truth, and Being Free*

Dear Reader,

It's Monday morning and the weather isn't so pretty outside. It's foggy, wet and cold. Your body screams to stay in bed, wrapped up in a cosy blanket and not moving any more than you must. The bed is a warm and luxurious shelter in winter. It can become a cosy haven.

Add a cup of coffee or tea, a nice book, fluffy socks and soft pyjamas and it's a recipe cut right out of hygge.

Now, as you embrace these words, start stretching a little bit, right and left, just like that. A deliciously sensual stretch. And now, wake up. I may be an ambassador for radical self-care, but it's a tool to support you to live your best life. But that best life will not happen all wrapped up in blankets. It's Monday morning, it's a new week. That means you have so many opportunities to write a new chapter in your book.

I'm sure that you, just like me, have gone through shorter or longer periods that felt uninspired. For me, losing that spark of inspiration led to anxiety and bursts of depression. But, after being fed up with having ashes where my fire should be, I rose up and thought: what is it I want to do? And in that place of no inspiration, no ideas, not knowing what to do next, it was indeed hard to hear that inner voice, my connection to the divine. Yet, in those darkest days, I started praying "Dear Divine/ Higher Spirit/ Goddess, I have no idea what to do, I'm totally lost. Please guide me." And then and there, I heard the voice "Just take the next right action." And the next right action wasn't about massive life changes. Nope. It was about waking up in the morning. It was about taking a shower. It was about healthy food choices. It was about not giving up on myself.

And here comes radical self-care. In that timespan, I had to take some days off to sleep in and catch up on rest, to read books and watch movies, to nurture that lost me. And I kept praying for yet another right action that I'd be able to translate in a step. And day after day, they came in. I found out I no longer wanted to continue my job and that my fire had been put out because of overwhelm, because my workload was just unmanageable. So, I chose myself. And when I made that choice and when I set resolutions for a life in which I'd be choosing myself first, things started falling into place. Not all at once, and not with a five-year plan. But with little puzzle pieces that slowly but steady, showed me how I can spark that fire yet again and piece by piece, a way out of the darkness was built. After being lost, even one step on the stairway back in to the light was enough for me.

So, dear Reader, I don't know you intimately, but I know you. I assume you also love feeling inspired, joyful and light-hearted, like the Universe doesn't have any edges. So, remember we were not put on planet earth, in our magnificent bodies (short, tall, dark-haired, blonde, a little fluffy around the edges, really skinny, wonderfully beautiful) to live a life that is less than WOW! We were given these bodies and all our limitations, thought patterns, families, to be born, to kick and scream like little rock stars and to heal ourselves enough to be able to live with zest, passion and experience incredible adventures.

Dear Reader, I'm not sure where you are in life or what pains or joys you are living, but always remember that in the darkest of dawns, somewhere a little further away from you, there is a treasure chest, just after the fog, which is just waiting for you to find it and open it up. A fantastic pirate's treasure chest, full of adventure, abundance, joy and inspiration.

Yeah, I know exactly what that sounds like. Remember, I've been through those tough times myself. But it is mandatory and necessary for each of us, just to not give up hope. Are you not able to trust yourself and your life right now? That's totally okay. Lean on the Divine, in whatever format or naming is comfortable for you. Just pray. Or meditate. Your feelings will guide you to what your mind and body need. A soapy TV show? There are great choices on Netflix. A sad drama movie? Tears are a wonderful healer. A hike in the woods? Nature has a wonderful grounding effect.

If you'll listen to these feelings and sensations, you'll also start hearing that inner voice that will become just a tad more courageous and which will start whispering at first and then become more and more loud, advising you on that next step. And then you, in the fabulosity that you are, will have the choice to listen and be brave and authentic. The magic will happen.

Boy, oh boy, it's not easy, I know. Especially when you're in a dark place, you get to ask yourself: how can I keep living with so much pain? When will I feel slightly better? Am I going insane? Is it natural for things to feel like this? But, yes, it is.

A few years ago, my father passed unexpectedly, and I was just out of college. Suddenly, I didn't just need to find a job, I needed to support myself financially. And I was in the worst depression. I asked myself all those questions. I didn't know whether I'd be able to make it. Had no idea whether there was a way out of that dark place.

But a little sparkly voice kept telling me to go on. And a while later, one piece at a time, things started falling into place. Little by little. I know I said earlier, that I went through another difficult time a while back, but eh, it's life, isn't it? We won't be able to feel the happiness without also feeling the sadness and we will not experience the feeling of success, without also going through failure.

Dear Reader, as I approach the end of my love letter to you just for today, and then for tomorrow, wake up. Get out of bed, put a nice outfit on and go rocking. You may be in a good place or it may not be the best time. Keep choosing yourself. If you're a woman, put on some nice lipstick and smile at yourself in the mirror. If you're a man, put on the best shirt and wear your sexiest aftershave.

Tonight, you can cosy back into bed, but that's not where the magic will happen. So, do whatever will make you feel the best for yourself, keep going out, keep rocking and I promise, that little by little, those puzzle pieces will start flying in.

With all my love, I send you the warmest hugs, sunshine and rainbows.

AN UNEXPECTED LEGACY

Kim Searle

Dear Reader,

It's Monday morning and I'm sitting here at the breakfast table, enjoying my three girls jabbering away, one-minute laughing, the next crying before suddenly remembering something and laughing again. It makes my heart burst with pride to watch them and the lovely women they've become, a real family.

It wasn't always like that. There was a time when they were always at loggerheads with each other as young adults. I'd begun to despair that we'd ever recapture the close-knit family we once were.

Because we were very close-knit at one time, not perfect, as life tends to be full of ups and downs, sadness and laughter, wins and losses don't you think?

A deep howl of laughter brings me back to the present and I look up at my eldest daughter regaling a story from her latest night out with her friends, and there are more shrieks of laughter. Not a bit like it used to be when I was 40.

Because, I was an 'older' mum at that age. I remember being so indignant about that, being called 'old' when to me I'd only just really got my life together. Of course, I can laugh about it now, as it turns out I was a bit of a trendsetter. *So many women these days waiting until their late 30s and even beyond to have children.*

I met my husband when I was 34, and our first daughter was born 18 months later, quickly followed by baby two and three!

I was a bit of rebel back in those days, so we didn't get married until much later (which was frowned on by our families), but I held very traditional views of how to bring up my children. One of which was to stay at home with them, but like any mum with three little ones under the age of five, it was tough.

We'd had to move away from both our families for work, and there was no family support on hand.

It was a good move though. We moved to one of those new towns, where everything was designed with families in mind, and it was so close to the sea. My husband was very sociable and made friends easily, as did I. We quickly became a well-known part of our local community.

Looking back, I can see now, that it was me who struggled to settle into this new life. I was fiercely protective of my family unit. I realise now, that this was the result of my own father dying young, and my mother re-marrying. I'd suddenly felt lost, ignored and unimportant. This was made worse, because my brother got all the attention. I saw him as an obnoxious sissy, whose every cry and whim was indulged. It resulted in much fighting and arguing. Yes, I became resentful and couldn't wait to leave home. MY life and MY family were going to be different.

As a family, we settled into family life and we soon welcomed baby number four, a boy. I was overjoyed about that. I'd always wanted a boy. Once he started school, money became so tight, I had to find a job that worked around school hours to help pay for the extras in life like clothing, outings, Christmas, and holidays.

But we were incredibly happy, 'The glory days' I call them. We laughed together, cried together, fought and played, partied and were a close-knit family. Holidays were in a camper van and it was all a very jolly adventure. We were lucky in so many ways, creating more happy memories than most.

But, I fought, laughed, cried and worked the hardest of all to create, achieve and maintain this. As a mother, you are mum first, cook, purse housekeeper, planner, nurse, counsellor, peace maker, wife and just like the big cat with her cubs, I was also the defender of all we had built.

My husband was the opposite, easy going, wanting everyone to be nice to each other, have a good time. He forgave easily, loved freely, whereas I didn't. We could have fallen out with someone in the morning, and he would be down the pub with them by evening. He was such a good dad; a great provider and he was very funny. It was hard in the beginning to stay cross with him.

But people learnt not to mess with me, I took no nonsense, even being known for throwing the odd punch or two. So different.

Inevitably, my children grew up, and became their own people. Only now as teenagers, it become harder to handle the rows and spats, with all the hormones flowing everywhere. But somehow on a Sunday, everyone would gather for lunch and everything seemed forgotten for a few hours.

Everyone loved my roast dinner, we'd always have 10 or more people around the table sitting on boxes and garden chairs. Strangers picked up by my big-hearted husband because they 'looked' hungry, the children's friends or partners. They were all welcome – I loved this side of family life. If they didn't do anything to harm my family, I could be as open hearted as my husband. Our reputation grew within the community as fun-loving people.

Ironically though not with our own generation, but with those of our children. We became a base for all the lost souls, the unwanted, the battered, the troubled. I took them under my wing, as the maternal side of me reached out to provide a haven.

Oh, and at weekends we had fabulous fun when we held one of our parties. Held after closing time at the pub, most of them turned into all-nighters. I would lay on a buffet, and everyone would come back, dance, debate, talk and drink. Anything could be called upon to be a celebration. Birthdays, promotions, engagements, it was Friday, all and any excuses.

Good times. But underneath, I can see now, that the things I tolerated as the children were growing up, became louder as they left home. My role was no more. I began noticing the differences between my husband and me. They began to irritate and chafe.

I now felt like I was taken for granted.

I was still working hard in my job to provide for the extras in life, whilst my husband had already decided he was retiring early and put his feet up. I was the one that dished up Sunday dinners every weekend, but no one seemed to invite us back. I noticed that the teenage angst had turned into 20-something disagreements, rows and arguments about who had done what to whom. My family were arguing with each other, and I tried to sort it out. The more I did, the more my husband seemed to let me get on with it.

I never learnt to not interfere. I just waded in, resulting in harsh words being said all round and some were deeply wounding, not just to each other, but for me. Once the fight was over, I became the one in the wrong. What was going on? I only wanted the best for them, and it was difficult to stay quiet. There were consequences brewing, I just didn't know it yet.

I'm not quite sure where it changed, even as I reflect on it now, but somewhere the children who were once very close knit and fought for each other, now just fought each other. They had not only grown up, but somehow apart.

Life and the universe have unexpected ways of lifting you, and it brought me grandchildren. They took me back to what was important for me, family, love, support and a kindred spirit. Children are so innocent and open, aren't they? Just wanting to be loved and I could give them that in bucket loads! So, for a time, the fighting and arguing was slipped into the background of life.

Time moved on, the grandchildren grew up or moved away, and this time, I found the emptiness I just could not fill easily. I realised gradually that I'd lived my life entirely for my husband and family. I no longer had value or felt important or part of anything.

Those seeds of anger and rage planted long ago were growing. How I felt I'd been treated over the years, by my husband and latterly by the children; the way my husband left everything to me, and always looked like the fun and loving one; the children blaming me when things didn't go right and my continual working to pay the bills, as my husband retired and sat with his feet up. It was beginning to take a toll.

I'd always smoked, in fact, I can't remember a time when I didn't, it was the fashionable thing to do. And I drank, not every day, but on Friday and Saturday nights, as there was no work the next day. The combination wasn't good.

I developed a wretched cough that was at its worse in the morning, it was 'smokers' cough, right? It didn't hurt, it was just irritating, so it never occurred to me to do anything about it. Oh, how I wish I had now, as I watch my daughters make yet another cup of tea, another family tradition.

Eventually, I was convinced to go to the doctors and get it checked out.

I don't know what I expected to happen, after all it had been going on for years, and I think the family just accepted it.

It was bad news.

I couldn't take it in – what was it the doctor said? Stage four lung cancer? What did that mean? What was the treatment?

It turned out there was no treatment, just a way of extending (more like prolonging) life.

Chemotherapy started immediately and I have never felt so ill in my life – it was like they were killing me one burst at a time. But do you know what? In a bizarre way, it was a turning point for me. I realised who was important in my life. How perhaps I'd got some things wrong. That all that effort I'd put in to raising my family had been worth it. Not only because they took it in turns to look after me, but as I began to appreciate who they were and their beautiful qualities and traits; their idiosyncrasies that made them who they were.

The rift between myself and my husband got wider, as he was in denial about it and expected everything to remain the same, wondering why I wasn't doing all the things I always did? I get it now, really, I do. But then I didn't, it turns out he was already developing Parkinson's. Right then, I was even angrier with him than I'd ever been.

I became weaker and weaker.

Taking more and more medication.

The inevitable was in sight.

As I sit here looking at the girls, I now can see things so much more clearly than before. Hindsight is a wonderful thing, don't you think? I realise that all my anger and frustration from my early childhood, coloured my adulthood. I'd aimed it directly at others who I felt were threatening what I saw as a great family unit, including my husband.

We never really spoke about stuff like that – so he didn't know what I wanted from him, more support, more love, more appreciation.

I regret that now, that somehow, I had not appreciated what I had, only what I'd lost. The overriding need for a loving, supportive family where I could belong taking over my ability to love and be loved more freely.

But all that is past, there is nothing I can do about it now.

There are no tears, for what might have been, here in this moment. Only a profound sense of joy as I watch my daughters, seeing them happy, settled and sorted. A deep unconditional love for the way the families they have created based on what they'd experienced. I'm so proud to have left a legacy of family, full of fun, and laughter for my wonderful grandchildren and future generations.

It seems the girls have finished their tea and are beginning to grab their bags and coats, saying goodbye airily, busily rushing off to the next thing.

I'm now here on my own and the silence is deafening. My mind moves to my death.

It wasn't a peaceful one.

Oh, it wasn't the pain from the cancer that was the problem. It was the party spirit we had fostered so much over the years spilling to my bedside as I lay there. The whole family together, doing their best to cope in the only way they knew how – to laugh and joke, chat, come and go, just like today at the table with the girls. I did eventually leave, in the quieter hours of early morning, as they sat around my bedside, silent, exhausted and pensive.

As I hovered above, looking down at them, I now appreciate just how much I was loved. It had never occurred to me how much of a real difference my husband and I had made to so many lives. Not just my family's, but those other kids who used to come to me and tell me their problems. I'd created a sense of belonging that had been absent from my own childhood. This was something to be proud of, an unexpected legacy of my life.

I come every Friday and Saturday to watch over what my family are doing, how they are getting along, it fills me with even more joy and happiness.

Let me leave you with this, as I, too, leave for another week. Sometimes it's hard to look at your life objectively in the moment, you're too wrapped up in what's going on. It's difficult to appreciate the bigger picture that is your life and the impact you have on those around you.

But if you can, make time to smile at something that is beautiful in your day. Share a few words of kindness for a stranger and those experiencing difficulties. Love with a wild abandon, knowing that you, too are loved by someone or some people. Appreciate those that are important in your life, it's so easy to take them for granted, but a well-placed thank you, or hug can make all the difference. And know that you don't know the journey that everyone has been on that has brought them to this point in time. So be, most of all just be.

Because it is only later looking back can we truly see the patterns, links and synchronicities that lead us all through this journey called life, helping, supporting and loving.

ABOUT THE AUTHORS

Jackie Frazier

Greetings, I am Jackie Frazier. I am a wife, mother, grandmother, aspiring writer and massage therapist along with a host of other titles. I live in South-eastern Kentucky in the gorgeous, breath taking Pine Mountains, a ridge of the Appalachian Mountains where I walk and seek a more spiritual life. You can find me here: https://mymagickalcabin.com/

Sandra ten Hoope

Sandra ten Hoope is a Corporate Governance and Compliance lawyer and blogger based in the Netherlands. She obtained a Master of Laws from the University of Amsterdam.

When Sandra was 4, she taught herself to read. And after reading through the children's section of the library three times, she turned to literature targeted at adults. At the tender age of 8 (and motivated by her experience as a child of divorced parents) she chose to read a series called 100 Questions About Various Legal Subjects—the first volume of which was on the topic of divorce. Her inquisitive young mind and curious heart fell in love with the ins-and-outs of the law. And from that moment on, she decided that she would work toward a career in the legal field.

Sandra has always been a highly-organised person, and this served her well while working as a corporate lawyer and team leader in the fiduciary services industry.

While Sandra's mind is stimulated by the analytical and detail-oriented nature of the law, her true passion is people. She is a connector and communicator at heart and is amazed by the capacity of human beings for creativity and innovation.

In 2016—as a labour-of-love side project— Sandra co-founded Relabel Rebels: a blog aimed at dissatisfied professionals who want to re-evaluate their careers and revamp their personal lives.

Sandra´s current focus is on the launch of her book Do Not Try Him at Home – which will be published by The Quiet Rebel Bureau in November 2019. In one of her previous relationships, Sandra endured domestic violence. Do Not Try Him at Home is aimed at showing people in a rather tongue in cheek way how to look out for narcissists and other guys you truly do not wish to allow in your house or life. Show-casing a number of archetypes (the NarcisSix) and with references to survival and healing aides.

You can reach Sandra at:
https://www.facebook.com/DoNotTryHiMatHome/ or
https://medium.com/@sandrariosvitaltenhoope

Wendy Radford

Wendy Radford is an experienced and qualified holistic therapist & spiritual mentor. She is vibrant and conscientious with a passion to encourage people to step onto the path of creative change, to re-awaken their lives to the beauty, passion, joy and laughter that brings her so much love of life. She understands that who you are matters profoundly. Being excited with you when you have that light bulb moment, she keeps you focused on the light that life brings and that which shines out from.

You can find out more about Wendy and how you can work with her at: http://www.radford-holistictherapies.co.uk/

Martine Bolton

Martine is a personal development consultant based on the south coast of England, offering training, coaching, hypnotherapy and Neuro-Linguistic Programming (NLP). She believes that effective thinking skills are the foundation of all results in life and in business, and that everyone experiences an element of faulty and/or unhelpful thinking that gets in their way.

Martine is passionate about helping individuals and organisations to achieve their goals and improve the results they are getting by cleaning up their thinking – enabling them to become happier, healthier, more successful and more prosperous.

You can connect with Martine at: https://www.linkedin.com/in/martine-bolton-513907155/, https://www.facebook.com/martine.bolton.9 and martine.bolton@sunshinedevelopment.co.uk

Kate May

I have been working as a professional tarot reader & psychic medium for many years in the U.K and more recently the U.S.A. I am a mum of 2 very active boys, and I run a psychic development centre within my spiritual coffee shop, the Mystic River Lounge in Portsmouth, UK. Within our centre, we host regular mediumship demonstrations, Workshops, and Spiritual based coffee mornings

I have been interested in all things spiritual since childhood, where I would talk with my Nan on the afterlife and playfully read the tea leaves together. My studies over the years, have taken me on journeys through astrology, numerology, tarot, spiritualism, paganism and angels.

I now teach tarot with astrology, psychic development and the Lotus Chakra - heal yourself within - course, plus I run several large Mind Body Spirit fayres across the UK. I have written for several online magazines doing tarotscopes and articles on spiritualism, plus interviews with well-known global mediums.

I work with other mystics on a fun online site - Loose Mystics. It's a live group of us mystics, working together, having weekly online discussions on spirit and all things mystical with live participation and online live readings.

I travel to different spiritual centres and churches doing tarot, astrology demonstrations plus talks across Hampshire, UK. Several times a year, I work in California doing readings, demonstrations or talks, and I have worked on psychic cruises and weekend psychic shows doing readings and workshops. Throughout the month, I work in London at Selfridges with the Psychic Sisters, owned by

Jayne Wallace.

I have been blessed to help many people over the years with both guidance and clarification from the tarot, and by bringing comfort through mediumship and working with Spirit. I am available for one-to-one readings, parties, face-to-face and online or Skype/phone reading plus talks and workshops.

You can find me at www.katemay.co.uk

Sarah Robinson

Sarah Robinson is a yoga and meditation teacher based in Bath, UK. She runs classes, workshops and retreats in the UK and abroad. Her background is in science; she holds a MSc in Psychology & Neuroscience and has studied at Bath, Exeter and Harvard University. Through work with yoga, meditation and the Goddess Temples of Glastonbury and Bristol – she found herself drawn toward a love of combining science with spirit, myth and magic!

You can read more about her adventures with the Goddess and yoga work at www.sentiayoga.com and Instagram & T333witter as @sentiayoga

Charlotte Chase

Charlotte is an Independent Consultant with Arbonne International. A vegan, pure and botanical health, beauty and wellness company. She is passionate about empowering and helping others to grow in self-belief and confidence and also to create the lives they dream of. She is a huge advocate of the Network Marketing Industry as she sees it as the business of the future and that it allows people to step into their best selves and lives. She is also very much into continuing to develop as a person, her connection with Spirit and the Universe to show that others can show up as their true selves. You can find her on Facebook at Charlotte Chase - Be You To The Full or on Instagram @charlottechase_aic

Zechariah Perry

I'm a holistic mental health practitioner, using lived experience and motivational approaches to empower individuals on their path to recovery. People can and will recover. Firm and unwavering belief is the powerful tool. I've been investigating ways in which formal mental health professions can look towards the healers working in local communities, as experience is the route of all strength.

Katie Oman

Katie Oman is an author, psychic and coach. She is the writer of three books to date including her latest Happiness: Make Your Soul Smile, which was published by O Books in 2018. She writes on a monthly basis for the UK national magazines, Soul & Spirit and Chat It's Fate. Katie has also used her own psychic abilities to help hundreds of people to gain the guidance and insights they've been looking for. Katie is a mum of three children and is based in Norwich, Norfolk. You can find out more details of her work at http://www.katieoman.co.uk

Kris Seraphine-Oster, PH.D

Kris is an author, brand strategist and marketing copywriter who teaches creative, spiritually-inclined entrepreneurs how to bring in more clients, customers and prosperity.

But actually, she's here to revolutionize the feminine face of business.

Once upon a time, Kris was a corporate marketing director and lead website developer for some pretty big names, including Citrix Online, E! Entertainment Television, Disney, ABC, Paramount Pictures.

While working full time and raising a

vivacious daughter, she attended Pacifica Graduate Institute to study mythology and depth psychology with such luminaries as Marion Woodman and James Hillman. With Ph.D. in hand, Kris began her quest to create a business that would uplift other entrepreneurs and trail blazers.

Since then she has helped hundreds of entrepreneurs create a business and livelihood that feels pleasurable, alluring and that reflects their authentic vision.

Kris is the creator of Higher Ground: Practical Magic For Women Entrepreneurs, a worldwide mentorship group and marketing/branding course where she provides daily feedback and strategic advice to women business owners.

She is the author of Return to Enchantment: Your Guide to Creating a Magical Livelihood, which swirls together archetypal psychology, mythology, case studies, and reflections, providing a practical and inspirational guide for entrepreneurs to create unforgettable marketing and branding that stands the test of time.

Her current writing project, Unbound is due for release in February 2019. Unbound will be a book and a companion licensing program for coaches and teachers who want to use Kris' methodologies in their own businesses.

You can find out more about Kris and what she does by visiting her website: http://www.mythicrhythm.com

Lynn Meadowcroft

My name is Lynn Meadowcroft and I love to inspire people. I live in a beautiful village in the countryside surrounded by mother nature. I have 2 wonderful sons, Sam and Billy who I love so much. I am divorced and have been for about 20 years.

My passion is to share with others the wisdom and teachings of Louise Hay as her work has inspired me so much and since applying her teachings my life has changed dramatically. I love to work with women who are ready to totally honour themselves to be seen, heard and valued in all areas of their life.

Nothing gives me more pleasure than to work with people and see their 'aha' moments and watch their transformation. It makes my heart sing.

My background has always been doing something to help others; I have worked with alcohol and drug addicts, homeless young people, families who struggled and I am still helping people but in a more empowering way.

I also run a ladies networking group; Unique Ladies Wigan and will soon be running unique Ladies Bury, again helping and supporting women in business.

I am a Reiki Master teacher, holistic therapist, Wise earth Ayurveda practitioner and Certified Heal your Life teacher and coach. I love the work I do and the people I work with. I run workshops, retreats for women, work with charities, work with businesses and offer one to one coaching.

To find out more please visit my website at www.lynnmeadowcroft.com. You can email me lynnmeadowcroft@googlemail.com

Ben Hornsby

Ben Hornsby is an entrepreneur, motivational speaker, and wellness & abundance coach. He specialises in helping others find self-love, overcomes addictions, regain health and find inspiration for life. Ben uses his own story to help motivate, inspire and guide others to find a path to self-love, joy and abundance. You can join Ben at his Facebook group, Feel the Fear and Embrace your True Self - https://www.facebook.com/groups/42242566 1426704/

Joy Andreasen

Joy Andreasen has been receiving messages from the world of Spirit for most of her life, but she began using her gift to bless others for the last twenty years.

She combines her training in spirit messages, mediumship, shamanism, Reiki, Numerology and various belief systems to bring healing and comfort to her clients through varied and personalized sessions that are never identical and completely guided by her communication with the Higher Wisdom she channels.

In recent years she began posting a daily message from Spirit based mostly on the cards of the tarot on social media. She also posts messages from Spirit on her blog and on social media when guided. You can reach her via her website: whispersofjoy.net

Melinda Annear

Melinda Annear is a Systematic Kinesiologist, Healer and founder of Chrysalis Kinesiology based in Fareham, Hampshire.

You can find out more about Melinda and her practice at:
http://www.chrysalistransformation.co.uk, https://www.facebook.com/ChrysalisKinesiol ogyMassage/ and
http://instagram.com/melinda_annear

F.A.W.

My story is a true story of both pain and the beauty of life. In my late 30s, I realised that I had been carrying a secret inside of me all my life. I was an incest survivor. Reading a news article about Jimmy Saville I had my first flashback. It turned my life upside down. I have a long way to go to complete my healing. The darkness of depression and anxiety come for me regularly, but I am grateful to be able to find my way out to the light each time. In doing so I am gradually uncovering the truth of what happened, and the truth of who I really am. I haven't been able to share any identifying details as there is an ongoing police investigation which will hopefully end in taking my abuser to court for what he did. I can be reached on email at author.hiddenchildren@yahoo.com

Luke Voulgarakis

My name is Luke Voulgarakis and I am now living my greatest life as a Yoga Teacher. I took the plunge to leave my full-time employment as a HR Manager in 2018 when my husband and I adopted a little girl, and I wanted to focus on doing something that really connected with me and allowed me to spend more time with her. I want to set an example to her that anyone can follow their heart with enough belief. Really, I just scratched the surface of my story, so if you'd like to find out more about me, you can find my business on Facebook & Instagram @LVYogaFareham or my website www.LVYoga.co.uk.

Paul Elliot

You can connect with Paul on his Facebook page: https://www.facebook.com/miepaul54/

Phillipa Clark

Philippa Clark – A Shining Light who's passionate about working with mind, body and soul. She's a therapist who uses a mixture of counselling, hypnotherapy and Rahanni Celestial Healing to help people who are feeling lost, empty or overwhelmed. Whether it's anxiety, fears or sabotaging habits holding you back, she can help you.

Philippa also offers soul realignment, which helps you understand more about yourself at soul level and past life regression so you can experience your past lives In addition, she's a Tropic Skincare ambassador as she's passionate about using natural products that are not only great for your skin but the world too. Philippa works from her own private practice in Lee on the Solent.

You can learn more about Phillipa and her services on her website: www.ashininglight.co.uk

Kate Buxton

I was born in Holland, grew up in London and spent time in America and Switzerland during my school years. After school, I did a BTEC first in mechanical engineering, alas it wasn't meant to be as I caught glandular fever. I took to working in shops, cinema, and theatre front of house. I've been a support worker to adults with learning disabilities and I've worked in pubs, which was very transient until finally settling in sunny Southsea. I've even had my own pub in Southsea, that wasn't meant to be either as a major illness, cancer, had other ideas.

After a few dodgy relationships and said major illness, a son later (15), two cats and two dogs, I married my lovely husband Rob. Sundance traditional pier shop with a modern twist was born about 6 years after I decided I really ought to do something with my psychic gifts. Based on South Parade Pier in Portsmouth, I offer Fairtrade clothes, accessories, gifts, Native American beading and the making of shamanic crafts and drum bags. I also offer spiritual healing of various types, and tarot/angel card readings. I'm currently working towards qualifying as a shamanic practitioner in 2019.I have been filmed doing cards for a TV series with a lovely friend. I have several other projects in the pipeline for this year, they remain top secret for the moment so watch this space!

You can find out more about me at http://www.sundanceshop.co.uk/

Renee Furlow

Renee Furlow is the Founder of Catch A Falling Star. She is a certified oracle card reader, crystal specialist, and an accomplished author.

Renee is a proud mom to her son and cats, a

writer and poet by nature, an eclectic whimsical creator, a specialist in Earth-Based spirituality, a graphic designer, a Goddess lover, an eCourse & eBook addict, a believer in affirmations, a renegade mystic, a magic inspire-er, an essential oil collector, a quote connoisseur, a stay at home maven, a loving but tough soul, and a mixed-media art and picture aficionado. Throughout Renee's journey, she has been blessed with incredible gifts and has learned some amazing lessons. Because of this, she knows that she is meant to share these blessings with everyone that she can.

Genevieve Robson

I am a medium, healer and teacher working in Hampshire, England. I work from Havant Healing and Holistic Centre near Portsmouth as well as at other venues in the UK. I particularly enjoy teaching the development circles and workshops that I run in Havant and Southampton. I am particularly interested in helping the students to connect with their Guides so that they can best serve and help others. I also carry out one to one psychic, mediumship readings and healing.

Find my events on
www.facebook.com/GennysGifts/

Alternatively you can find me at
www.facebook.com/Havant-Healing-and-Holistic-Centre and www.havanthealing.co.uk

Susan Thames

Susan Thames is a moon and star gazing, nature loving wild woman that lives on a precious bit of heaven in Northeast Texas. A druid, a crystal healer, an herbalist and a magic maker. She is also the creator and caretaker of a quaint brick and mortar herb and tea shop named StarDragonfly Herb Company.

https://www.facebook.com/StarDragonflyHerbCompany

Michelle Rene

Michelle Rene explores life's perplexities in her blog, Pen Umbra's Conundrums (https://penumbrasconundrums.com). A graduate from the University of Arizona with a BA in English and a minor in technical writing, she occasionally lets literature and science play muse to her creative process. Currently, Michelle is working on a book of poetry through the lens of the physical, emotional and spiritual effects of having endometrial cancer.

Michelle has two adult children, two cats and resides in northern California. Her day job in local government as an animal services administrator often includes herding kittens and people. When not writing or working, Michelle loves to spend quality time kayaking with herons, bald eagles and osprey.

Reba White

Rebecca "Reba" White is an artist and writer. Her work can be found in Soul Path Magazine, her personal blogs, Quiet Rebel, and gracing homes and offices of family and friends.

Reba lives in Arizona with her sister, a loving marmalade tabby, and a midnight cat from hell. She is a warrior fighting a battle against lifelong depression and anxiety, and a cheerleader for perseverance. It is Reba's hope that through her writing and art, she can touch lives, and help others who have similar battles.

"Depression is a bitch, but you can't let it win! Keep fighting!"

Diana Sass

I'm Diana Sass, from Romania, a spiritual kid continuously looking for her tribe. I'm trying to integrate spirituality into my day to day job, where I'm actually a corporate bunny.

At my job, I analyse business processes and define ways they can be optimised and together with management, plan mid- and long-term strategies on how best they can be implemented and controlled.

Yes, I know exactly how sexy that sounds. Still, to be true to myself (not that being a strategist isn't one of my callings), when I wake up in the morning, I read positive affirmations and pull out tarot and oracle cards for myself. When I'm disciplined, I also meditate. I trust the way of the Goddess and I choose to believe in more gods than one.

I believe with all my heart, that you can be both. I can analyse the trends in the tarot cards and then go out and be all business and professional. It doesn't have to be one or the other. Never. We have to choose ourselves. Always.

You can learn more about me and my thoughts by visiting my web page: https://discorporate.wordpress.com/

Kim Searle

Kim Searle was born in Hampshire UK and spent most of her adult life working in the IT & Telecoms sector. Her heart though, has always been with people, providing a shoulder to cry on, a sympathetic ear for those going through tough times in life. It was only after her own life traumas caught up with her, that she went onto qualify as a Cognitive Hypnotherapist, NLP Master Practitioner, Coach and Spiritual Practitioner. Kim is now working for herself and positioning herself as an Emotional Health Guru. Her first book Midlife is NOT a Crisis, based on the processes she has used with clients and herself to help them heal and let go, is an Amazon best seller.

Find Kim at www.kimsearle.co.uk

ABOUT THE QUIET REBEL BUREAU

If you're a mind-body-spirit author or entrepreneur, you hold a vision greater than self-publishing a book or running a business. You want to make a difference.

You want to help others achieve more from life. You want to share your gifts and be of service. You want your unique voice and your wisdom to be heard.

Your own business – a traditional business, an online business or the business of being an author – is a vehicle to get your message into the world, to do what you love AND make money doing it. At the Quiet Rebel Bureau, we want to help you reach these goals.

We work with spiritual entrepreneurs to help you:

- self-publish books
- get more from blogging
- create an authentic digital presence
- gain clarity & direction in your business

Find out more at
https://quietrebelbureau.com